THE ACCENT OF
LEADERSHIP

THE ACCENT OF
LEADERSHIP

WORDS MATTER

STEVE KELLY

WINTERS
PUBLISHING GROUP

Published by Winters Publishing, LLC
2448 E. 81st St. Suite #4802 | Tulsa, Oklahoma 74137 USA

Book design copyright © 2014 by Winters Publishing, LLC. All rights reserved.
Cover design by Affari Project
Interior design by Caypeeline Casas

Published in the United States of America

ISBN: 978-1-63122-803-2
1. Religion / Christian Life / Personal Growth
2. Religion / Leadership
14.06.06

CONTENTS

THE ACCENT OF LEADERSHIP

Then they would say to him, "Then say, 'Shibboleth'!" and he would say "Sibboleth" for he could not pronounce it right. Then they would take him and kill him at the fords of the Jordan.

Judges 12:6

The accent of leadership is distinguished. The leaders of God's kingdom speak with a noticeable accent. They use words of life, and they speak with one voice. Men and women who understand the power of the accent of leadership and the power of their words can accomplish great things for God. Those who do not will eventually be discarded; they simply don't sound right.

The accent of our native country dwells in the heart and mind as well as on the tongue.

—Francois de la Rochefoucauld

THE ACCENT OF LEADERSHIP IS DISTINGUISHED

I often introduce myself as the most Australian-sounding American anyone could ever meet. I was born in Queens, New York. My family moved to Sydney, Australia, when I was eight years of age, and I lived there until I was thirty-five, when I moved back to America with my wife and our three children. At some point soon after arriving in Australia, I lost my American accent. As a young boy in a foreign country, I desperately wanted to belong; I wanted to fit in with the culture of this new world. Early on, I became frustrated that I would often say words that people didn't understand, or I would use expressions that were not common to the people of Australia. It felt as if every time I said something, the people around me made a comment about my American accent. I didn't want to be known for my accent; I wanted to be known for being myself.

I don't know if I intentionally attempted to change or if I merely adopted the sounds that I heard as my own, but over time I developed an Australian accent. Language experts state that usually accents are easily changed up until a person reaches his early twenties.[1] In my case, it was a relatively easy adjustment, as I was still a young boy when we moved to Australia.

The irony of the experience I had upon moving to Australia is that when I returned to America over twenty-five years later, I received the same reaction from Americans as I had experienced as a boy in Australia.

Everyone commented on my accent. It distinguished me from the crowd. From the moment I met the baggage handler at Los Angeles International Airport, to a conversation with the flight attendant on our way to Virginia Beach, everybody noticed my accent. I handled their attention much differently as a man in my early thirties than I had as an eight-year old boy. This time around, I had matured. I was comfortable with my voice.

In order for me to change my accent back to that of an American, according to linguists, I would have really had to *want* to change it. It would have required a diligent effort to change my accent because I had become fully mature. This time, however, I did not desire to change my accent. I liked being distinguishable from the crowd. I enjoyed the fact that my accent disarmed the people around me. Most importantly, I no longer was as insecure as I was as a small boy, and I realized that I did not need to change my accent to be accepted. In fact, I soon discovered that my accent was one of my strongest influencing attributes. My accent distinguished me, and as a result, people instinctively wanted to hear what I had to say.

THE ACCENT OF LEADERSHIP IS NOTICEABLE

It should be clear by now that my accent is one of the most noticeable attributes of my outward persona. As I mentioned, our accents are much easier to change when we are young. In both the natural world and in spiritual leadership, our habits and characteristics are easy to shape in the early days. As we mature, we become stiff, even rigid. If a person doesn't grow up speaking with the accent of leadership, or isn't exposed to the accent of leadership as a young individual, the effort required to adjust our voice to one of leadership is more challenging. It does not come easily. But it is well worth the effort.

When we came to America, my children had Australian accents. My oldest child and only daughter, Alyssa, was ten, and my two sons, Josh and Sam, were eight and five, respectively. I got to witness in them what I had experienced as a boy moving to Australia. In a matter of weeks, the boys had lost their Australian accents, but Alyssa worked hard to keep her Australian accent. In part, Alyssa tried to keep her accent because just before our departure from Sydney, pastor Brian Houston, during our last service at Hillsong Church, made her promise in front of the whole church that she would keep her accent! Such is the power of an accent—it marks a person and identifies where they are from, to what place they belong.

From the moment a speaker opens her mouth, the audience can tell where she's from by her accent. As long as Alyssa spoke with an Australian accent, everyone in America recognized that she was from another country. In time, even Alyssa's accent changed, because she was daily surrounded by people who spoke with an American accent. Because she was still young, it was easier for her to adapt, and before long, she took on the accent of the country that was now her home.

Your accent is a major distinguishing part of who you are and the culture to which you belong. Before coming to America, some of my Aussie pastor friends said to me, "We don't know how it's going to go for you, whether America is going to receive you because of your Australian accent." They were concerned that I would be ostracized or even rejected because I didn't sound like an American. My experience has been the exact opposite.

One great example of the benefit of my accent is my typical shopping experience. Because of my accent, I get better service, or at least more attention from the sales clerks. The shopkeepers are used to hearing American voices all day long, and so they may be tempted to ignore those customers. But when I speak, it's a different sound. My voice attracts attention. The sales clerks always look up and ask me, "Where are you from?" or "Are you Australian?" Which typically leads to the question, "What are you doing here?" And I get the opportunity to answer, "I pastor a church." No American pastor or leader who sounds American gets those questions asked of him, but I do often, and I use it to my advantage. I have a moment to tell them who I am, where I'm from, and what am I doing here. Then I'm able to invite them to church. Having a different accent can clearly be an attractive tool for reaching people who would otherwise have been disengaged or reluctant to have a conversation.

THE ACCENT OF LEADERSHIP SPEAKS
WITH LIFE AND AUTHORITY

The advantage of my accent is clearly demonstrated by that simple example. When I speak, people know that I'm from another culture, from another place. I am an American citizen. I have an American passport. Yet I sound like I'm from somewhere else.

I believe the same principle is true when it comes to the kingdom of heaven. Jesus was a leader, and Jesus said in John 6:63, "My words are spirit and life." Jesus said in John 10:10, "I come that you might have life and that you might have it more abundantly." Whenever Jesus spoke, he also spoke with great authority. He spoke with authority, because he had the power to speak life into every situation. He had authority over the wind and the waves. He had authority over demons. Ultimately, He spoke with so much life that He had authority over the grave. When He said, "Lazarus, come forth," a man who'd been dead for three days arose and walked out of the tomb![2] Jesus' words come through his mouth, but they originate in His spirit. They are more powerful than the material world, for they created the material world.

The Bible tells us that the power of death and life are in the tongue.[3] When we speak, we ought to speak like Christ spoke. We ought to speak like we're from another culture, another kingdom, and our words ought to carry weight. They should have authority. Our words will have influence for either life or death. They ought to transcend this natural world and bring the reality of the spiritual world into this natural world. Jesus taught us to pray, "Thy Kingdom come, Thy will be done on Earth as it is in Heaven."[4] He intended for the words we speak to bring the life of heaven to earth, to bring life to dead situations. Just as Jesus' words brought the dead to life, when a leader speaks, the tone of his or her voice carries the power of life and brings authority to disordered circumstances.

THE ACCENT OF LEADERSHIP REQUIRES FLUENCY IN THE LANGUAGE OF GOD'S KINGDOM

This chapter presents a simple question: "Do you speak with the accent of leadership?" We all speak with a physical accent. This question is not about whether you have a southern drawl, a laid-back California tone, or speak with a Cajun dialect. In order to have great conversations, or inspire people in their native language, you must be fluent. Fluency is the ability to function smoothly, without hesitation or interruption. In order to be fluent in any language, a person has to use it continuously. In order to have the accent of leadership, we have to be fluent in the language of God.

The Bible says that the followers of Christ are not of this world.[5] We are in it, but we are not of it. We are just passing through: we are pilgrims, we are strangers, we are aliens.[6] The Bible tells us that we belong to another kingdom, to another culture. We are citizens of a place not of this earth. When you speak, does your accent identify you as belonging to the culture of heaven, as being a citizen of the kingdom of God? Do you bring that accent everywhere you go? Not just by speaking with certain colloquialisms of the church world, but everyday, everywhere you go, do you speak with life and authority?

Is your accent distinguishable from the accent of the world? Is the way in which you speak unique when compared to the expressions used by those in this world that do not believe that Jesus is the Messiah? Every time I open my mouth, everybody knows I'm not from America. Every time a Christian leader opens his mouth, people in the world ought to recognize that this person speaks differently from everybody else. People should hear that there is an accent; there is an inflection to the tone of the statements made by a Christian.

The response of the listener should be, as it is for people hearing my Australian accent, "He's not from here," or, "I want to know where she's from."

The accent of leadership is not just an audible tone; it's also the expressions that are unique to the kingdom culture. Again, from my natural experience, even now when I return to Australia with my family once a year to visit, there are certain expressions that Australians have, slang words and idioms that I begin using again. These are expressions that have no relevance in America but are used everyday in Australia. My wife and I instantly recognize them from growing up in Australia, but my children don't understand them. My children have spent many years in America now and have no regular exposure to the Australian slang words.

Most Americans have heard the expression, "Throw some shrimp on the barbie," and understand that *barbie* is a shortened way of saying barbecue. But some of the less familiar expressions are "She'll be apples," which means things will be all right, or "mystery bag," which is slang for sausage. Isn't that a good one? I love the way Australians tell it like it is. These expressions would have no meaning unless you were familiar with the culture and the conversations of Australia. There are other expressions that are more vulgar which, if said in Australia, would get a person in trouble, but in America they don't have the same meaning. Likewise, there are slang Australian expressions that have a negative connotation in America but have an innocent meaning in Australia.

And so, when we are in Australia from time to time, my sons will hear us speak the slang of our Australian friends, but they don't understand us. Even though they are our sons, they do not share our culture, because they've been immersed in the American culture and form of English.

I remember one time we entered a crowded elevator and Sharon said, "Wow, this elevator is chockers!"

Our son, Josh, turned around, and in a very American accent asked, "Mom, what is chockers?"

Sharon and I took for granted this term, which means "chock-full" or "chock-a-block." She was just saying how full the elevator was.

Another time I offered Josh and Sam some *sangers*, which is an Aussie slang for sandwiches. Their confused look reminded me that the things I took for granted were not shared with my children. This experience is a reminder that the accent of leadership is one that must be intentionally formed, and the language of leadership must be trained. Just because you grew up thinking and speaking a certain way, does not mean your children will automatically understand or even be familiar with what you know intuitively.

My boys try to adapt to the culture, but they aren't familiar enough with it to be fluent. Therefore, they sound out of place and out of tune with the people around them. Similarly, when Christians aren't familiar enough with God, when they don't spend time surrounded by the power of the kingdom culture and they don't regularly speak with the language of life and authority, they lose the accent of leadership. They try to speak with authority and power, but they end up sounding clumsy, awkward, and insecure. We can't communicate effectively if we're confused and delayed while attempting to translate our thoughts into a foreign language. We can't lead unless the accent of leadership is authentically our true voice. We can't lead unless we are fluent in the language of God's kingdom.

Sometimes I'll travel to other parts of the world, and as I make a point in a sermon, some of the people will say, "Oh, that's an American thing you're saying, that's an American gospel." By this they mean that I'm making a point that they believe is only relevant or effective in American churches. I preach the gospel of Jesus Christ without apology and without reservation. When I hear feedback like those who think I sound too "American," I'll always explain that we cannot allow our national identities or cultures to get in the way of a kingdom culture. Though I'm proud of my American citizenship and am thrilled to live in the most historically significant region of the United States, I am first a citizen of the kingdom of God. Before we're citizens of the earth, before we're American, Australian, English, African, Indian, or Russian or whatever country we call home, we are all first citizens of heaven. The citizenship of heaven must be the predominant culture in our lives and must always take priority over our earthly citizenship and culture.

THE ACCENT OF LEADERSHIP IS ARRESTING

The accent of leadership that comes with our citizenship of heaven is powerful; it is so distinct that it should stop people in their tracks. It should be arresting. In John 7, the story is told of a time that guards were commanded to arrest Jesus but they could not—instead, his speech arrested them!

> Finally, the temple guards went back to the chief priests and Pharisees, who asked them, "Why didn't you bring him in?"
>
> "No one ever spoke the way this man does," the guards replied.
>
> John 7:45-46

Imagine the scene. The Pharisees and priests were furious about the influence of Jesus. His accent of leadership was causing a sensation and a revolution among the people who believed in Him. The people who were turning away from the leadership of the Pharisees and were listening to Jesus exasperated the Pharisees. So, they ordered the guards to go out and arrest Jesus. This troop of well-trained, fierce soldiers arrived at wherever Jesus was (He would have been easy to find—Jesus' incredible accent of leadership drew crowds no matter where He went). Perhaps the soldiers had to work their way through the throngs of people who had gathered to hear Jesus.

Maybe as the guards were moving closer to Him, they too could hear his powerful voice, his distinguishable tone, and his words of life and authority.

By the time they reached Jesus, they had heard His incredible accent of leadership; they were convinced that He was truly not of this world. Perhaps they realized they didn't have the authority to arrest Him. Because he spoke with the accent of heaven, they didn't have the legal jurisdiction to make a charge against this man. Whatever happened that day, we know that the soldiers returned to the temple priests, their bosses, with a mission *unaccomplished.*

It's important to note that these soldiers chose to disobey their command. I live in a fantastic military town, and if there's one thing I know about the military life, it's that a soldier *must obey* the command of his leaders. The consequences of disobedience are significant and can even lead to a dishonorable discharge from military service. In this case, the Roman soldiers were risking much more than a dishonorable discharge. It's possible they risked their very lives by choosing not to arrest Jesus!

It was very common in that day for men to make a life-long commitment to serve their nation by joining the military. The vow to serve came with an automatic subordination to the rule of the centurion who commanded a soldier's assigned platoon. Any command handed down was to be fulfilled completely, directly, and accurately. If they left any portion of the mission uncompleted, ruthless consequences often followed. The penalties varied depending on the severity of the infraction; however, the most common forms of correction included public humiliation, the most ultimate form of degradation in Roman society, and the infliction of pain.[7]

With this knowledge I believe we can infer that a soldier charged with the duty of arresting Jesus who then failed to do so could quite likely receive the harshest punishments of that day. Many Roman soldiers, at the hand of their centurion, would be beaten with a leather and metal whip, causing critical blood loss, and sometimes severe muscle damage.[8] Additionally, a general in the Roman army had the authority to sentence a soldier to death for failure; although there is no evidence to prove this occurred in this case, it's not out of the realm of possibility.

Understanding this reality makes the soldier's decision all the more shocking! How powerful must have been the words of Jesus that not just one soldier, but an entire team of trained military men forsook their command and risked certain punishment and possible death rather than take captive the Son of God!

Maybe the guards thought that this would be the last time anybody would ever hear from Jesus again once they arrested Him, knowing what the Roman authorities and the Jewish leaders wanted to do with Him. So they listened to Jesus. The soldiers were so taken and captivated, so mesmerized with the words of Jesus that they ended up walking back to the post from where they were sent without Jesus.

The Pharisees asked one of the soldiers, "Well, where is he?"

And the soldier said, "Where is who?"

And they said, "Jesus."

He said, "Oh, that's right, (we couldn't arrest Him) never a man spoke like this man."

When you speak, are your words arresting? The guards were sent to arrest Jesus, but instead they were arrested by Jesus' words. As leaders, do our words captivate people? The Bible says that when we speak we should speak as the oracles of God.[9] We ought not to be an echo repeating what somebody else is saying; we ought to be an original, prophetic voice. If, like Jesus on the day those guards arrived, you were speaking and a hostile group arrived to discredit your leadership and your authority, would your words be so captivating, so arresting, that they would arrive at the same conclusion: "No one ever spoke the way this man does"?

THE ACCENT OF LEADERSHIP SPEAKS WITH ONE VOICE

The accent of leadership is distinguished. The accent of leadership brings life, and it speaks with authority. It is noticeable and arresting. Another important aspect of the accent of leadership is its inclusive nature.

The accent of leadership never uses words like "us vs. them" or "the powers that be." The accent of leadership uses words of inclusion, like "we". The accent of leadership never says things like, "Nobody ever tells me what goes on in this place." The accent of leadership takes personal responsibility for being in the know and does not blame others if they're not in the know. The accent of leadership speaks inclusively and is not seditious.

In Galatians 5:19-21, Paul compiles a list of the works of the flesh, among them sexual immorality, witchcraft, and idolatry. These are sins that most everyone immediately recognizes as wicked. But also listed among the likes of drunkenness and anger is a less common word, sedition.

As mentioned, I pastor a church in a military city. In fact, the region where I pastor has one of the largest American military installations in the entire world. Our proximity to Washington, D.C., and the port of Norfolk provides both the political and geographical reasons for positioning a massive military presence in our community. The military, perhaps more than any other faction of people, depend upon authority and the chain of command for success and indeed, for survival. Nobody understands the word *sedition* better than the brave men and women of the US Armed Forces. Sedition is deceitful, underhanded, and insidious. Webster's dictionary defines sedition as "resistance to or insurrection against lawful authority." Sedition is usurping and undermining. Sedition happens when a traitor gives the leader the impression that he is submissive but he's actually being divisive and disloyal.

A common way sedition occurs in church is as follows:

You might go to your leader with an idea—and you had a group of people already excited about the idea of what you wanted to do, and you went to your senior pastor or to your leader with permission to carry out this new initiative. You had discussed this new idea that you thought would be fantastic with a small circle of church members. You've already gathered a group of people around you and come up with a plan of what it's all going to look like, but when you go to your leader, your leader says, "I do not have a vision for that. I don't want that to be done."

Instead of accepting the authority of the leader, you take a personal offense, and you go back to the people that you talked to, and you say to them, "Look, we're not going to do this, because I spoke to the senior pastor, and he doesn't want it. And after all, he is the leader, so we're going to do what he says."

While that sounds very submissive, the Bible calls it sedition. When you go back to those people, rather than saying, "The leadership doesn't want it." You should say, "I've talked to him about it, and we feel like right now we need to put this aside and not worry about it, and we feel like there are other priorities." Use the word "we". Don't undermine or usurp your leader's authority in a way that shows false honor to your leader and actually attaches and endears people to you.

I experienced this with a volunteer who was part of our pastoral care team. His sole responsibility was to make hospital visits when I was unable to because of travel. Once, a member of the church left because she claimed to me, "No one visited me in the hospital. No one cares about me at this church!"

I asked the volunteer if he visited her. He told me he did visit and he sent flowers.

I went back to the upset church member. Her response was, "Oh, he visited me, but he's not a *pastor*. He's just one of my friends. "

I found out later that my volunteer was sending flowers, paid for by the church, but he signed the card as though they were from him. The point here is that he provided a compassionate benefit, but he did it in an inappropriate manner. He should have made the person in the hospital feel as though the senior pastor was there—and he certainly should have signed the card as coming from the church!

Don't act in such a way that you end up only being outwardly submissive. People will become resentful toward the leadership because when you fail to speak with one voice. Your leadership should not leave behind a damaged trail of people. It should not create people who were committed to a vision but became fractured and disillusioned because you were not able to speak in inclusive terms. The accent of leadership should connect people to the greater vision, to the big picture, rather than loyalty to your individual leadership.

THE ACCENT OF LEADERSHIP IN CHURCH LIFE

In our lives we have relationships that I consider to be divinely appointed God connections. Since 1999, many great friends and artists have come to minister at our church. One great God connection is with Darlene Zschech. If you don't recognize her name, it's very likely you recognize one of her songs—"Shout to the Lord."

Well, it was during the time that song was extremely popular that Darlene and the Hillsong Praise and Worship Team came to our church. During the same time we were expecting her arrival, the East Coast was experiencing a hurricane. We received phone calls from people all over the United States. Many people were eager to come to Virginia Beach to hear Darlene and the team from Hillsong Church. At the time of this particular event, our head usher was a retired master chief in the US Navy. As you might imagine, as a military man who was well trained, he took on the job of head usher with a sense of duty. He was a serious, diligent head usher.

Hillsong Church is globally known, and its worship music is sung in churches everywhere. As a result, whenever they came to our church, we had a packed house. I received a call from a church that was almost a day's drive away from us. This church wanted to bring a busload of people, but it was concerned about the availability of seating.

Of course, if they were willing to make the long trip, I wanted to make sure they would have a place to sit, so I approached our head usher. I said to him, "We got a phone call from a church that is a seven, eight-hour drive up the coast. They asked if they came down on a bus, could we please assure them that we would save them some seats so they didn't get turned away if the place was full. I don't know the church or its pastor personally, but we should be gracious hosts to this group." In my opinion, this was a reasonable request.

I asked this retired master chief, who was the head of our host team, "Would you make sure that forty seats are reserved for the people from this church who are driving eight hours on a bus, and save these seats for people to make sure that they have a place to sit in the service?"

Even though there was a hurricane approaching, we had a full house, and many people tried to sit in the seats that we had set aside for the group. And every time someone sat there, even though it said "Reserved," our head usher made sure they moved to another area. He did his job. The only regrettable thing that he did was every time somebody sat there, he would explain, "You cannot sit here. These seats are reserved for friends of Pastor Steve's, and you must move out of these seats now, because Pastor Steve has reserved these seats for friends of his, and so you need to move now."

Well, obviously, that's not a seditious thing to do, but I had to teach this man the accent of leadership.

Remember, the accent of leadership speaks with one voice and brings life. Though the head usher accomplished the mission, he spoke with a message that was not inclusive and did not bring life to the people around him.

People were hurt and offended by the way he spoke to them, and also resented the fact that he told them that they were seats saved for friends of mine. These weren't friends of mine; they were simply people who made a request that I was happy to honor. They were making a big sacrifice to come so far, and I wanted to make sure they had a place to sit when they arrived.

Unfortunately, anyone who sat in those seats was told to move because I was saving seats for friends, which only created resentment toward me by those people. I realized that I had yet to fully train our head usher to speak with the accent of leadership. Though his voice was distinguishable and noticed, it was incomplete. He spoke with authority, but he failed to bring life. He spoke in a way that was not inclusive. Had he explained that "we" had reserved these seats and helped the people find seats in another part of the auditorium, no one would have been offended, and certainly no one would have developed resentment toward me as the senior pastor.

This experience was a great learning lesson for me and for our team. Many times, we have some components of the accent of leadership, but we need to have the complete accent of leadership. We need to be fluent. We need to bring life. We need to speak with one voice.

DEVELOP THE ACCENT OF LEADERSHIP

1. Is your voice clear and distinct from the crowd? Do you unnecessarily worry about the opinion of the masses? If you were placed in a different environment, would you change your accent, or would you continue to speak as a citizen of the kingdom of God?

2. Do you speak with life and authority? Do you inject power and a positive voice in difficult situations? Are you speaking as an overcoming leader when others are crying out in fear?

3. Are you fluent in the language of God's kingdom? How much time do you spend surrounded by His thoughts and principles? How much time do you spend surrounded by speech, images, and thoughts of the world?

4. When leading others, do you speak with one voice? Do you present responses from your leadership in "us vs. them" terms? Do you speak with a language of inclusiveness?

HONOR

As snow in summer and rain in harvest, so honor is not fitting for a fool.

Proverbs 26:1

Honor is, in part, properly respecting a leader—not based on their title or position but on their character and leadership. Honor reduces the possibilities of a follower becoming overly familiar with his leader; however, the leader is responsible for establishing proper boundaries. When we fail to honor others, we lose regard for God's leaders. Honor is tangible; it is "weighty." When we give honor, we give weight to our leader's words.

Honor is the reward of virtue.

—Cicero

HONOR REDUCES THE HAZARDS OF
OVERLY FAMILIAR RELATIONSHIPS

This book is intended, in part, to expose and limit the effects of some of the errant teachings I have heard during my experiences of the past thirty years in the church. An important biblical concept that has been misunderstood, improperly explained, or outright abused is the idea of honor. Honor is repeatedly mentioned in the Bible. We read about honorable and dishonorable people throughout the Bible. We see examples of Christ himself being both honored and dishonored. My hope in this chapter is that the reader will gain a better understanding of honor's place in our lives and the importance of properly honoring leadership. Also, it is my desire that this chapter help leaders understand how to effectively establish the balance between isolation and overly familiar relationships in the leadership of the church.

After I received Jesus as my Savior and realized He was calling me to be a pastor, I enrolled in Bible college at a church about an hour's drive from Sydney, Australia. I was young, excited to be serving God and obeying His call for my life. I remember being taught in Bible college that pastors and leaders should never allow people to get close to us, because if they get close to us, they will become overly familiar and will lose respect for us. The support for this notion is found in Matthew 13:54-58:

> When He had come to His own country, He
> taught them in their synagogue, so that they
> were astonished and said, "Where did this Man
> get this wisdom and these mighty works? Is
> this not the carpenter's son? Is not His mother
> called Mary? And His brothers James, Joses,
> Simon, and Judas? And His sisters, are they not
> all with us? Where then did this Man get all
> these things?" So they were offended at Him.
> But Jesus said to them, "A prophet is not with-
> out honor except in his own country and in his
> own house." Now He did not do many mighty
> works there because of their unbelief.

My instructors explained that the people who knew Jesus were too familiar with him, which led to the people of His country becoming offended by His power. They were offended because they felt like Jesus was telling them how to live. The people of Nazareth thought, *Who does he think he is?* The attitude of the friends and neighbors who knew Jesus as a boy was similar to the attitude that sometimes accompanies the natives of an area that has seen mostly poverty or an absence of success. When someone begins to excel and is promoted, the people in that community can become offended, because it makes them feel like failures.

As a result of that teaching, I saw an attempt by many pastors to avoid any close relationship with the people in the church. This approach can lead to dangerously unrealistic expectations by the congregation. Church members begin to think, because they are never close to the pastor, that he is infallible or something more than a human being. While I absolutely see the biblical truth and the consequences of allowing people to become overly familiar with a pastor, I think that truth taken too far causes pastors (particularly senior pastors) to live very lonely and isolated lives. Some of the senior pastors I know who were devoted to this idea of avoiding any close relationships would take it so far that they refused to have friends in ministry. This distortion of a few verses about Jesus' hometown has led to numerous burnouts and breakdowns among pastors around the world.

In order to avoid this, pastors should have the freedom to be themselves, in and out of the pulpit. Of course, if the pastor is covering up sin in his life, he can't expect to remain in the pulpit forever. One way or another, it will come out. But if a pastor believes he simply has to be "holy" twenty-four hours a day, seven days a week, he will eventually crash. Pastors are human. One of the great lessons I learned about the balance of a pastor-church member relationship came from observing Pastor Brian Houston.

During my time as the director of Hillsong College and as the senior associate pastor at Hillsong Church, Pastor Brian helped me identify and overcome the improper teaching I had received. His day-to-day leadership showed me how to reconcile receiving honor and maintaining personal relationships without allowing people to be overly familiar, which could thereby diminish my role as a senior pastor in the church. He always said if a pastor is not the same person outside the pulpit as he is in the pulpit, that pastor will not keep the respect of the people. He also taught that a leader should not be lonely. Leadership should not be an isolated life. As you build a team, you ought to build it with the people you relate to, you work with, and you enjoy.

I remember also being taught in Bible school that as a pastor and a leader in the church, if a preacher was preaching and you felt any need to respond to an altar call about something that they preached on, that we were not to go forward to receive prayer, because we should never let people see that we have problems. Much like the teaching on not having friends from among the congregation, this notion was based on a belief that if people see a pastor's humanity they may not respect his leadership.

The reality is nothing could be further from the truth. I think Jesus showed us this by choosing Peter to be the rock upon which the church was to be built. If ever there was a leader who revealed his humanity, the tempestuous Peter was it. He was rash, impetuous, emotional, transparent, brazen, and passionate. All the qualities that would be considered poor form in the circles I traveled during my early years as a pastor were the very same characteristics that enabled Peter to be Christ's *only* choice as the foundation of the early church. Those attributes also correspond to being faith-filled, determined, loyal, active, bold, and willing to do whatever it takes for the cause. People need to know that their leader is not a cold, robotic saint. They need to see him or her overcome challenges with appropriate transparency.

This section presents two critical aspects of pastoral leadership. Boundaries in relationships with the congregation are important and necessary, but isolation will lead to a pastor's eventual deterioration. It is important that the pastor be clear with the people from the outset that he can't be everyone's best friend, that he is human and will make mistakes, but that he is God's set man with a call to build the church. The balance of respect for the man of God and his ability to be himself in and out of the pulpit is essential to growth and allows the people and the pastor to have a healthy, productive, long-lasting relationship.

FAMILY IS DANGEROUS WHEN IT DOESN'T SHOW HONOR

The degree of application for this leadership truth will vary from person to person. Some pastors are naturally more of a "people person" and could hang out with people in the church all the time without jeopardizing the people's respect. Others need more private time. Regardless of your style, it's good to have some non-negotiable boundaries, and it's also helpful to look to examples in the Bible that give a clear violation of this leadership truth. A pointed example can be found in Numbers 12. In this chapter, Miriam and Aaron come to Moses and complain about Moses' wife. They make a critical statement in verse 2: "Has the Lord indeed spoken *only* through Moses? Has he not spoken through *us* only?" (emphasis added). They chose to speak what essentially amounts to rebellion. They placed themselves on the same level as Moses, and the Lord heard them. The Bible makes clear in multiple passages that God appoints leaders, and no man can elevate himself, nor can another man replace him unless God does it.[10] God was so angered by Aaron and Miriam's disrespect of Moses that He came down to set them straight!

> Suddenly the LORD said to Moses, Aaron, and Miriam, "Come out, you three, to the tabernacle of meeting!" So the three came out. Then the LORD came down in the pillar of cloud and stood in the door of the tabernacle, and called Aaron and Miriam. And they both went forward. Then He said, "Hear now My words: If there is a prophet among you, I, the LORD, make Myself known to him in a vision; I speak to him in a dream. Not so with My servant Moses; He is faithful in all My house. I speak with him face to face, even plainly, and not in dark sayings; And he sees the form of the LORD. Why then were you not afraid to speak against My servant Moses?" So the anger of the LORD was aroused against them, and He departed. And when the cloud departed from above the tabernacle, suddenly Miriam became leprous, as white as snow. Then Aaron turned toward Miriam, and there she was, a leper.[11]

God appointed Moses as the leader of Israel. When He heard Aaron and Miriam speaking against Moses, God showed up. He called all three of them out and explained in no uncertain terms how unique Moses was, and He defended Moses as His most important servant. Then He left, and Miriam had leprosy! Later in the chapter, Aaron asks Moses to pray for Miriam to be healed, and God heals her, although He does so reluctantly. He even requires her to leave the camp for a week to serve a solitary confinement. Aaron and Miriam were seeking co-equal leadership of Israel. They believed they were the same as Moses and that they had the right to tell him whom to marry. Without a doubt, this is an example of unwarranted familiarity, and God shows how much he despised their behavior by coming down immediately, scolding them and leaving Miriam with leprosy.

There are also New Testament examples where we see the problem with people becoming overly familiar with leaders. Similar to Aaron and Miriam with Moses, Barnabas challenged Paul's authority and believed he might stand as his equal. In Acts 15:36-41, Paul wanted to go back to visit the churches, and Barnabas insisted that John Mark be included with them. Paul would not allow John Mark to join them, as Paul believed John Mark had demonstrated a failure to persevere earlier in their ministry. Barnabas was unable to abide by the boundaries of leadership that Paul set in place, and as a result, they parted ways, and Silas joined Paul in Acts 16. We do not know the full consequences for Barnabas, but he is never again mentioned in any sense of ministry, and in Galatians 2:13, Paul writes, "and the rest of the Jews played the hypocrite…so that even Barnabas was carried away with their hypocrisy."

I might be pushing the envelope a little bit here, but I also think of when Jesus was twelve years old and Mary and Joseph couldn't find him. They searched for three days, and the Bible says they were anxious, as you can imagine.[12] Finally, they found Him in the temple, astonishing the priests with His insight.

Mary, as a concerned parent, asked Jesus, "Where have you been? Didn't you know we were worried sick about you?"

Jesus replied, "Did you not know that I would be about my Father's business?"

This exchange is unusual, and yet Jesus was not being disrespectful to His earthly mother. He was reminding her that, even as a twelve-year-old, He knew who He was, that she knew His purpose, and she should remember Jesus' real Father was God. Mary was overly familiar with her Son. Often it's family that can be overly familiar and inappropriate in the conversations they have with a leader's people, because the family member may have "changed his diaper," and they remember when the leader was just a child.

The danger of Mary's overly familiar comments and the people from Nazareth's response to the life of Jesus is they became offended by His success because they knew him too well. If a leader becomes too familiar the potential exists that the people will stop respecting the gift and the leadership. I often joke about my own family and how my younger sister loves to, in a humorous way, point out to people who know me how she's known me my whole life. And she loves to say, "Let me tell you about the real Pastor Steve, the Steve that I knew, that I grew up with."

Now I'm going to tell you myself so that my sister doesn't get the chance!

Like all young people, from time to time my siblings and I did not get along. And I freely admit I did some terrible things to my sister. I made her eat Ford pills, which are a laxative. I once accidentally threw a dart, and when it went into her foot, I put my hand over her mouth and made her promise—before I took the dart out—that she wouldn't tell Mom or Dad. And she was begging me to take the dart out, but I said, "I'm not taking it out until you promise me you won't tell," because I knew I would be in trouble. Now, of course, that's a family story, and we all laugh, but people love to try and hold you down and remind you of your foolish mistakes of the past. My sister loves to tell that story because it reveals immature behavior and perhaps reduces my esteem in the eyes of other people.

People love to hold you back to who you once were rather than who you are today and the person you are becoming, and it becomes a moment of being overly familiar. Pastors who have family members in their church need to navigate this situation carefully, as nobody is more familiar with you than your own family.

In Australia, we call the attitudes exhibited by Jesus' family the "tall poppy syndrome." We rejoice when somebody gets successful, but if they get too successful, we want to cut them down to size. In America, it's called "crabs in a barrel." If you place one crab in a pot, he'll get out of the pot. When two crabs are placed in a pot together and the first one tries to get out, the second crab will pull the escaping crab back into the pot. We are not crabs, and we can't afford to be pulling people down.

We need to be lifting people up and encouraging people. That's honor. Honor is rejoicing in other people's success, in other people's prosperity, and weeping with those who weep. Honor shows empathy. We should rejoice with those who rejoice, we can weep with those who weep, and we must make sure that we appreciate the people that God has put in and over our lives and give honor where honor is due.

THE LEADER IS RESPONSIBLE FOR DEFINING THE BOUNDARIES

Leaders are responsible for creating the boundaries in relationships so that people without discretion aren't able to inappropriately expose a leader's weakness. A leader must also not take himself or herself too seriously. There is a balance between the concept that "love protects," which can sometimes be used as an excuse for avoiding constructive feedback and an overly critical spirit. [13] If a leader does not properly manage relationships at the outset, he will potentially end up with either a group of advisors that are merely "yes men" or at the other extreme, advisors who make his life a nightmare by constantly complaining and second-guessing his leadership. Either scenario ends in isolation.

I do not believe that a leader cannot get close to his people. But, it is the leader's duty to engage people and manage expectations. I think leaders create many of their own problems and get upset with people for being overly familiar, but I think we create those problems when we don't draw the lines of how a proper pastoral relationship develops and operates over time. In the end, it's the leaders that will be called by God to account for how they've managed the hearts and minds of their people.[14] When the leader correctly manages the relationships by setting and keeping proper boundaries, it is easy for people to show honor.

In a workplace setting, over time, people can become overly familiar with their co-workers or their supervisor. The job is supposed to be a place of productivity and professional behavior. And the way colleagues can talk to each other sometimes is dishonoring because they are treating the relationships as too common; they're taking it way too casual. However, it is the supervisor's role to establish the culture of honor in the workplace. If you are not the supervisor, but you work in an environment that is too casual and is actually dishonoring, take it upon yourself to show honor. You will gradually see a change in others, and you will honor God by honoring your fellow worker.

During the past thirty years, I have had the privilege to help train many young men and young women to serve the Lord, and many of the young men have not had great, strong father figures. With the current high divorce rate in our world, a lot of these young men come from broken families, and they are looking for a father figure, and they look to me as their dad and want to please me. I sense it. I know it. I feel the weight and the responsibility of that. And sometimes in leadership, you need to bring correction and direction into a young person's life, and they find it hard to handle that correction. They've never had a strong male authority figure in their lives, and they find it hard to handle discipline, and they take it personally, and it becomes a challenge to them to accept correction and grow. Because of the life experience, they often treat me as their dad, and they struggle to distinguish between my pseudo-parental role and my role as pastor, and I realize it's up to me to help draw those lines. I can't expect them to draw those lines, so I have to help them.

I think of one particular young man who just wanted to be part of our family. He wanted me to be his dad. And he got to the point where he would come to our house and not even knock at the door. He would just walk into our home as if he was a family member. And we had to say to him, "You've been overly familiar here. You can't just walk into our house. You're not part of our family. And if you're going to come to our house, you need to knock at the door and wait for someone to let you in. You've crossed the boundary. You've been overly familiar."

When I was the director of Hillsong Leadership College, I would, of course, enjoy interacting with the college students, and I might see one and walk up and give them a little thump on the arm just as a moment of recognition to say hello to him. And he would smile, I'd smile, and we'd all laugh about it. On one occasion, I was walking through the offices in the Bible college, and I was escorting the Sydney North Assemblies of God District with our executive. I was walking through the college offices, and one of the same students came up and tackled me while I was walking with a group of distinguished visitors. He crossed a boundary. He thought it was funny. Rather than get upset with him, I realized that I had to draw the boundaries for people to teach them not to become overly familiar. It is the leader's job to help them understand the right time and the right place to do things, and it's up to the leader to draw the boundaries.

HONOR IS BASED ON RESPECT, NOT A TITLE OR POSITION

When the leader fails to set the proper boundaries and the people become overly familiar and even disrespectful, one of the natural responses by the leader is to declare the power of his position.

Years ago, when I was a pastor and elder at a church, there was another pastor/elder on the staff who faced this challenge. This leader struggled with getting the support from staff members, and he would come to me and say, "Don't people know I'm an elder in this church?"

I would joke with him and say, "Obviously not. Would you like a neon sign? And when you wear it around the office, it will light up 'Elder,' and we'll just call you Elder Fred so everybody will know that when you speak, you need to be listened to—you are somebody important."

Obviously, this leader misunderstood the process of earning honor. I had fun teasing him, but the consequences of failing to gain respect by virtue of who you are rather than your job title are very serious. A leader doesn't gain honor from the people because his nametag says "Elder Fred." A leader gains honor when the people respect him. There are no shortcuts. Honor is gained through a lifetime of integrity and consistency. One great test that I believe is a way to measure the quality of a leader is to have honest conversations with the leader's staff. When the people closest to a leader respect him the most, that's when you know the leader is doing it right.

I've often heard people ask pastors, "What should we call you? Should we call you pastor? Should we call you reverend? Should we call you bishop?"

The best answer a pastor can give is, "You can call me anything you want, but if I don't have the anointing of God, people aren't going to follow."

Too many leaders get caught up with the desire to be honored. They focus on outward behaviors and measures of respect. They draw boundaries hoping to create respect artificially, and then they adjust the boundaries endlessly in a mechanical effort to feel adequately honored. In the end, the leader experiences greater isolation because he keeps pushing the people further away. As he prevents people from getting close, he misses out on real friendships and great blessing.

HONOR IS TANGIBLE; IT GIVES WEIGHT TO A LEADER'S WORDS

The word *honor* is similar to the word *tribute*. We show honor when we give tribute to a person. In days gone by, tribute was the word used for taxes. A person showed honor to his king by paying tribute. They honored the king by paying him something of value. If tribute was not paid, a person was considered to be dishonoring the king. Today, we can still show honor by paying tribute to our leaders.

When we attach worth to our leader's words and leadership, we honor him. We dishonor a person when we fail to attach worth to their life. We dishonor our leaders when we treat their life and leadership as common or ordinary. We should never dishonor people by treating them as common. All people are precious in the eyes of God, but He specifically *commands* us to honor our leaders. The Bible says that they who lead in the house of God, those who teach and preach and do it well are worthy of double honor.[15]

Not only are those who minister worthy of double honor, the Bible also teaches that the builder of a house is worthy of more honor than the house itself. In comparing Christ to Moses, the author of Hebrews writes, "For this One [Jesus] has been counted worthy of more glory than Moses, inasmuch as He who built the house has more honor than the house." It is important to never forget the builder of a work of God by honoring the man or woman of God.

The Bible also says we are to honor the Lord with our wealth, which leads me to believe that one measure of honor is demonstrated by our financial contributions to the leaders God has placed in our church.[16] If honor is demonstrated by tangible assets like money, it is quantifiable. Your willingness to show honor and the magnitude of honoring another is measurable. If you review your financial contribution statement at the end of the year, you can make your own determination about how much you honored God and your leaders by your giving to God's house. Honor is not just something you do in your heart or with your words. Honor is demonstrated by contributing tangible substance to the recipient of your honor.

The word used for honor in the Old Testament Hebrew is pronounced "ka-vode." *Kavode* means to be heavy, to be weighty, or to have great substance. When we honor somebody and when we honor the Lord, we give substance to their words. We show *kavode* by allowing what they say to be heavy in our lives. The words of our leaders carry weight, and we allow them to "weigh in" on how to live a better life. When we honor the Lord, we allow God's Word to weigh in over our own thoughts and feelings.

My own children are now at an age where they can make their own decisions, but they still honor me by allowing my opinion to influence their choices. They allow the words that I say to carry weight in their life. They show me true honor by giving value to my advice at this stage in life. When they were little, they had to give weight to my words or they would be punished. That was simple obedience. When they heed my suggestions now, they are showing honor.

The same is true with God's Word. The same is true with our employers. It's one thing to obey when there are direct consequences. It's another thing altogether to show honor when we have the option to make our own decisions. We honor, and that honor is tangible. It's not just lip service. It's something that is demonstrated by whether we allow the words of our leaders to influence our lives.

HONOR IN CHURCH LIFE

An overly familiar attitude toward a leader can create many challenges in church life. People become presumptuous upon a leader's time and talents. They no longer properly respect leadership. They see their senior pastor as a friend more than they do a man of God. I remember one time in our church one of our pastors—who was friends with a volunteer leader in our church, as was I—and this particular volunteer leader began to say things about me and about the church that was just crossing a line. He had become overly familiar and was beginning to speak critically, and his conversation was totally negative about aspects of my leadership.

And so one of our pastors, who was also this guy's friend, challenged him on it and said, "I don't believe you should be talking like that. I don't think that's showing respect and honor, and I need to challenge you on it." The volunteer leader became offended. And the pastor was calm but did not adjust his correction, because the reality was that the leader had spoken out of turn.

In developing leaders, it's essential to remember that regardless of the gifting or resource that a leader brings to the church, the standards and expectations for honor never change. If it's allowed to fester and grow, it will become contagious and will lead to an unhealthy environment for both the pastor and the congregation.

As time passed, I began hearing the same things from this key leader, and I finally challenged him and said, "Listen, this pastor spoke to you about your attitude and your lack of honor."

He responded by saying, "But I was just talking to him. He's my friend."

And I said, "Listen, he's a pastor, and he's a pastor before he's your friend. He's a friend, and he's your pastor, and you must always honor who he is as a pastor before you turn him into a friend. Don't treat him as something common. And if he's challenging you about being negative and about being critical, it's not that you're having a conversation just with a friend, but here is somebody who is a spiritual authority, a spiritual oversight, who's seeing something in your life. And because you're treating him as a friend, you're not respecting what he's saying, and therefore there's no openness to be challenged and to be accountable and to change."

In this situation, over time, he improved and understood the value of proper honor and respect for spiritual authority. One of the recurring expressions in our church that I repeatedly share with our pastors and staff is "Don't blame them; train them." This principle is especially true in the area of proper honor.

As society has grown less formal, the church has reflected that. In many areas, this relaxed attitude has brought more people into the church that otherwise would have avoided it because they were intimidated by the solemnness of the service. However, we cannot allow honor to be diminished for fear of offending someone. It is a truth of leadership that has been critical for building God's house since the beginning. Leaders should manage the balance of familiarity and honor by setting the boundaries of acceptable behavior and never compromising the value of honor. By keeping it a priority, the spirit of respect for God and His house will elevate the entire church to new heights of service and commitment.

DEVELOP A LIFE OF HONOR

1. Do you show honor even when no one will notice? Does your leader know that you honor him or her? If you are a leader, have you properly defined and modeled honor for your team or employees?

2. Have you ever been overly familiar by making inappropriate jokes or comments at the expense of your leader? Have you asked for forgiveness? Do you seek opportunities to demonstrate proper honor among your peers? As a leader, have you taken the time to think about and implement proper boundaries without isolating yourself?

3. Is your life an example of honorable behavior? Do you believe that honor is the reward of attaining a position or title? Do you seek to honor God and others, or is a personal platform and "ministry" your primary focus?

4. Is the weight of honor apparent in your life? Do you give weight to the Word of God by truly implementing its counsel in your life? Do you give your leaders' words weight, or do you fail to respond when a challenge or correction comes from your leader?

THE RESTRAINTS OF THE VISION

Where there is no vision the people cast off
restraint.

Proverbs 29:18a

Then the Lord answered me and said: Write the
vision and make it plain on tablets that he may
run who reads it.

Habakkuk 2:2

A compelling vision ignores the voices of those who say
it can't be done. A compelling vision will provide the
necessary restraints for the fulfillment of that vision.
The restraints of the vision are necessary, for they give
us the boundaries of self-discipline and the pathway
to achievement. The restraints of the vision will always
include submission to the big picture. Without a vision,
the people cast off restraint. With the right vision, the
world is won.

The only thing worse than being blind is having
sight but no vision.

—Helen Keller

A COMPELLING VISION IGNORES
THE VOICES OF THOSE WHO SAY IT CAN'T BE DONE

A compelling vision can produce powerful motivation, which can lead to exceptional achievement. A compelling vision is an essential foundation for anything great that we accomplish. How we act on that vision is called motivation. Human beings are naturally motivated by internal desires as well as external inspiration. Vision is the fuel that fires the intensity of our motivation.

In recent years psychologists have proposed a theory that attempts to identify and quantify the power of motivation and its connection to a "vision." Known as Self-Determination Theory (SDT), this theory states that mankind has three major needs to satisfy: (1) self-determination, (2) competence, and (3) relatedness.[17] E.L. Deci and R.M. Ryan wrote an overview of this theory in the 1985 textbook entitled, *Intrinsic Motivation and Self-Determination in Human Behavior*. Since then, numerous other books and research articles have been written on SDT in a number of human activities. In essence, SDT proposes that people engage in an activity because (1) they chose it and have a natural interest in it; (2) they have an ability to perform that activity and want to display competence; and (3) the activity deepens their connection with the people that are important (to them) in their community.

I am not a psychologist, and this book is not intended to discuss the merits of various psychological theories, including SDT. However, SDT does correlate so directly with the contents and purpose of this chapter that I felt strongly motivated to include a brief discussion of SDT and its potential ability to explain why people will wear the restraints of a compelling vision. In my own words, Self-Determination Theory says that almost everyone wants to excel in something they believe they are good at, alongside others they care about.

I believe this is how Christians should be positioned within the body of Christ, as manifested on earth through the local church. In the church we find people with all sorts of talents and gifts, and it is part of the role of the pastors and leaders of the church to help people find their part. In the New Testament, Paul writes to the church at Corinth and provides an excellent description of this God-ordained structure.[18]

When the church is aligned under the leadership of a compelling vision to reach the lost, to heal the broken, to feed the hungry, and to love their neighbor, extraordinary achievements can be accomplished. Miracles can happen. When each member of the body of Christ is able to excel in an area of service to which he is interested and competent, alongside others with the same passions and talents, the components of SDT, the church will flourish, and many more will come to Christ. This is not to say that SDT is a church growth philosophy—far from it! There is nothing that man can add to the message of Jesus. As Christ said, "And I, if I am lifted up from the earth, will draw all peoples to myself."[19] This brief illustration from the field of psychology is merely meant to draw a comparison between studies of the connection between a compelling vision and human motivation and the greatest vision of all time, the kingdom of God and the most powerful motivation ever, saving a soul.

SDT has been studied in great detail in the realm of athletics. It has a natural application to sports in general and athletic competition in particular. In researching for this book, I discovered many studies and research articles on SDT and its explanation for success in the Special Olympics, the Paralympics, and the Olympics. It is interesting to note that while reading, I discovered that *intrinsic motivation* is one of the key elements in all of the elite athletic competitions. *20* Intrinsic motivation comes from within; it does not depend on external encouragement. In fact, it often helps an athlete overcome external *discouragement*. One of the puzzles for sports psychologists remains an explanation for why some athletes excel in the face of adversity, while others flounder without repeated external encouragement. This attribute is directly correlated to an athlete's level of intrinsic motivation.

Likewise, in building the church, in reaching the lost, many Christians face external discouragement. We must rise above the voices that tell us we are foolish or naïve, or worse, delusional. We must not give credence to the external comments or rejection that might offend our natural man. We must be intrinsically motivated by the knowledge that God has given us a compelling vision that requires discipline, growth, and internal strength to accomplish. We must be like the Olympic athletes who have a compelling vision and ignore the voices of those who say it can't be done.

A perfect example of this principle is the success of Michael Phelps, the world-famous US Olympic swimmer. He had a vision to win multiple gold medals at the 2008 Olympics. He even expressed his ambition to win eight gold medals, an unprecedented accomplishment. While he was training for the Olympics, several of his predecessors—highly accomplished and respected swimmers—said there was no way he could win eight gold medals. One of the great swimmers from Australia, Ian Thorpe, claimed that it was physically impossible. In an article published in The London Telegraph (August 5, 2008), Thorpe said, "I have said before that I don't think he can do the eight (gold medals)…it's sad, but I just don't think it will happen."

Some athletes might have been allowed those comments to negatively affect performance. After all, Thorpe is one of the great swimmers of all time. He won three gold medals in the 2000 Olympics and won six gold medals in the 2001 World Aquatic Championships. Perhaps the negative statements by a respected peer would have weakened the resolve of a lesser athlete. Indeed, Phelps claimed in his book *Beneath the Surface* that he idolized Thorpe as he was growing up.[21] Yet because of Michael Phelps's powerful intrinsic motivation, rather than question his vision as a result of Thorpe's comments, he took the newspaper clippings that quoted the former swimmer and placed it in his locker.[22] Each day he read the criticism and became even more motivated to see the vision of eight gold medals achieved. He was so internally determined and restrained by his desire to be the best that even the voice of his idol was ignored because it didn't line up with his compelling vision.

A COMPELLING VISION PROVIDES THE RESTRAINTS TO ACHIEVE THAT VISION

Michael Phelps did not allow criticism to push him off his vision. In fact, he used those comments as additional motivation, as an opportunity to show the outside world that he could do the extraordinary. Driven by this vision, he was restrained from wasting time, from loafing or relaxing more than he should. Perhaps when everybody else was asleep, he was doing laps. When everybody else was playing, he was paying the price in the pool and in the weight room. He disciplined his diet and his lifestyle; he restrained his appetite against anything that diluted his ability to achieve that vision. He was willing to forego temporary enjoyments or "down time" in order to achieve an extraordinary performance in the 2008 Olympics.

And guess what? He did it. He accomplished the unbelievable feat of eight Olympic gold medals because his compelling vision provided him with restraint. Not only did he overcome the critics, equally as significant in his quest, he overcame his own natural desires. He refused his flesh; he controlled his body and trained it so that he could perform at peak levels when it mattered most. His compelling vision gave him the self-control necessary to do the work, because the vision was so much more compelling than any temporary pleasure he might have experienced if he chose to relax during his training regimen.

Intrinsic motivation is essential, because if a person is only motivated by external encouragement or reward, he may end up faltering if no one is cheering him on, or when he is tired, isolated, or bored. Galatians 6:9 (NKJV) commands us, "And let us not grow weary while doing good, for in due season we shall reap if we do not lose heart." We must have the internal passion and drive to ignore our critics, and just as importantly, to ignore our own flesh. Throughout history and in the Bible, we can find examples of men and women who fell short of their potential because they allowed their flesh to overcome the vision of something greater.

In the Old Testament there are examples of people who had extraordinary opportunity but lost it because they could not control temporary urges. In Genesis 25, the Bible tells us about how Esau forsook his birthright because he couldn't think past his next meal. Esau had been out working and was hungry. When he entered the house, he smelled some good food being prepared by his brother, Jacob. He asked Jacob for some food. Jacob knew Esau's shortsightedness and took advantage of the moment. Jacob said, "If you give me your birthright, I will give you this food."[23] Esau tragically could not see past his next meal. He didn't know how to delay gratification. He literally gave up his inheritance (and his family was wealthy) for a bowl of soup!

Hebrews 12:16 says that Esau is "profane" and "godless" for trading his birthright for "a morsel of food." His momentary inability to restrain his flesh for a greater vision landed him in the New Testament, thousands of years later, labeled an "infidel." He was more motivated by his flesh than he was by a vision of what God had for his life, and he forsook what God had for his life because he did not know how to delay gratification.

Another tragic example of a man who had greatness within his grasp and sacrificed it for temporary pleasure is Samson. Samson was marked for extraordinary greatness. He had an angel announce his birth, and declare in Judges 13:5 that, "He shall begin to deliver the Israelites out of the hands of the Philistines." Only three other people in the Bible had an angel announce their birth: Isaac, the grandfather of the twelve tribes of Israel; John the Baptist, the cousin and herald of Jesus; and Jesus, the Savior of all mankind. If these were the only people who the Bible records had an angel announce their birth, it's safe to assume that Samson had a very significant purpose!

And yet, Samson never was able to deny his flesh and ultimately deny his ego in order to fulfill what God had planned for his life. He was explicitly given the restraints for his vision. He didn't have to guess if his "training regimen" was right or would produce the best results. He only had to keep the rules of a Nazarite. He had to follow three rules: (1) drink no alcohol; (2) eat no unclean thing; and (3) don't cut the hair. It seems to me that these rules are a simple request in exchange for being given supernatural strength and the opportunity to rescue one's people from an oppressive foreign government!

Ultimately, Samson violated two rules, and possibly all three. He initially failed to control his hunger for food and violated the Nazarite vow he was required to keep by eating honey from a lion's carcass.[24] Many scholars believe Samson may have violated the prohibition against alcohol when he hosted the pre-wedding feast in Judges 14:10. Of course, we all know that the last rule was violated when he instructed Delilah to cut his hair, and at that time, "The Lord had departed from him."[25]

Both Samson and Esau were unable to restrain their flesh and control their temporary desires. Though they should have understood the power of the compelling vision, they did not. They violated the rules and abandoned their restrictions, and they are forever known for accomplishing far less than they should have or could have in their lives.

THE RESTRAINTS OF THE VISION PROVIDE THE BOUNDARIES OF SELF-DISCIPLINE

The biggest difference between the illustrations of Esau and Samson and the accomplishments of Michael Phelps is the attribute of self-discipline. People with no vision do what they want, when they want. They fail to live a life of passion or commitment because the only priority in life is what feels good for the moment. Self-discipline is certainly not a priority for people with no vision. In some cases, even personal hygiene is not a priority! People without a compelling vision don't really have any goals; they lack ambition. They go to work when they need money to pay temporary bills, rather than working to build something significant with their life. They have no vision for their earthly life, and they certainly have no vision for the kingdom of God.

Without self-discipline, people abuse their bodies. If they had a vision for full health, they would make right choices about their diet and exercise. But when the self is undisciplined, behavior is uncontrolled. Without self-discipline, people have no restraint about what they eat or where they spend their money. If they want it, they want to get it now. People without self-discipline do not understand the principle of delayed gratification: they prefer to play now and pay later rather than pay now, play later.

Self-discipline is a consequence of vision. Self-discipline is not something that can be "added" to a person's life like buying a new pair of shoes to run faster. Self-discipline occurs through the recognition that the vision is greater than whatever temporary distraction or desire arises between the casting of the vision and its ultimate realization.

Some people mistakenly set a goal to simply have more discipline. Their thoughts run like this: "If I only had more discipline about how I spend my finances, what I do with my money, if I only had more discipline with my eating habits, if I only had more discipline with time, then I'd achieve…" Some people think if they just were more disciplined, problems would go away. Yet until we develop a vision that is bigger than simply being more disciplined, the change we seek will never become permanent. Of course we could easily excuse ourselves, especially if we were brought up in a family where discipline was not instilled as a child. When discipline is introduced in adulthood, it's a lot harder to build the right habits, as years of poor habits and undisciplined living have to be overcome.

Developing self-discipline as an adult is unfortunately something I had to do. I was brought up in a family that believed if you wanted to buy something, you just got a credit card. Over time, those habits led to uncontrollable debt. I remember as a young man having debts for foolish, unnecessary things. I was a teenager with a parttime job as a floor sweeper in a department store. I really wanted a new stereo. And my parents just said, "If you want it, you pay for it. You can go into debt for yourself." They didn't co-sign; they weren't a guarantor on the credit that I used to buy the stereo. This purchase started me on a path of buying multiple items on credit, making minimum payments, and building up debt for temporary pleasures. I never understood the power and importance of delayed gratification, of saving finances. As a result of that, it cost me a lot later to learn some of those disciplines that were never taught in my home.

As stated earlier, self-discipline is not something a person just adds to his life. It is not the absolute reason why people fail to achieve great things in life. I do not believe that an absence of self-discipline is necessarily the problem. What helped me overcome what was not trained into me at a young age was not the goal to be more disciplined, *but the goal to have a clear vision of what I wanted to achieve with my life.* And when I had a clear vision of what I wanted to see in my life, what I believed God wanted to do through my life, I became aware of the limitations that would hinder me from making that vision a reality.

With that in mind, I found the practice of living a disciplined life to be simple. Not easy, but simple. With a vision, you put on restraint. It's not the restraints, it's not the discipline—*it's the vision.* As Habakkuk says, write it down, make it plain. Once it's written down and easy to see and therefore follow, the restraints are easy to apply. It becomes a roadmap for transporting you from a position of frustration and repeated failures to a place of accomplishment. Self-discipline serves as the boundaries as you travel forward to your goal. The self-discipline becomes intrinsic because the vision is more compelling than any of the temporary pleasures that could prevent the realization of the vision.

Once I had a vision to get out of debt, I had a choice about where my money was going to go. Was it going to go for a new pair of jeans, was it going to go for the newest toy, or was it to pay off the debts? And as a result of having a vision, a clear vision for Sharon and myself, we became ruthless and determined about removing all debts out of our lives—first our various credit cards and charge accounts—and now we're focusing on our mortgage and believing God to have that paid off in half the amount of time that the bank has given us so that by the time we retire, we have the asset of a house. And because of the vision of a fully debt-free lifestyle and a fully un-mortgaged home in the future, we're wearing the restraints; we live with the self-discipline necessary to achieve that vision.

Everyone needs a vision for his or her life. For Michael Phelps, it was winning in the Olympics. For me, it was getting out of debt. For some, it's losing weight. For others, it's even more difficult, like beating a drug addiction. Whatever the vision is, it must be greater than simply having more self-discipline, and if it is clear and able to be followed, it will lead to success. The vision serves as the roadmap, and the self-discipline serves as the guardrails as you actually travel toward your destination.

A RESTRAINT FOR THE VISION WILL ALWAYS INCLUDE SUBMISSION TO THE BIG PICTURE

Once a person has identified the vision for his or her life, the next step is being strong enough to allow the progression toward achieving that vision to help build the church of God. For some people, this is intuitive. For some of the people reading this book, the notion of submitting a personal vision to the greater vision of the work of the church is a completely foreign concept. The truth of the matter is the single most compelling vision on earth is—and for every Christian should be—to build the church. The church is God's only plan to reach the lost and to redeem mankind. If a Christian does not have the local church as a priority, he is missing the whole point of his or her faith.

Christ proclaimed the plan of God when he told the disciples to go into every nation, to teach, and to make disciples.[26] Disciples are made in the church. Converts are trained and mature over time to be able to repeat the cycle, to go out and make new disciples, and thereby continue to build the church. In that process, there will come moments when every Christian leader will face the challenge of learning to submit his vision about the practical ways in which the church ministers, or even how the church service itself operates. These are matters of style, not substance. And yet, many times Christians allow matters of taste or personal preference defined as "vision" to interfere with their ability to follow what God is doing.

When I first came to Virginia Beach from Australia, I encountered a leader in the church, a brother in Christ, who struggled with submitting his "ministry" to the big picture—to what God was doing at our church. This man had been very involved in the church and was a leader within a para-church organization called Royal Rangers. Royal Rangers is a great ministry that mentors young boys through outdoor activities and physical exercise, coupled with biblical training and fellowship. They have retreats and national competitions that allow boys to develop great skills and self-confidence while learning how to lead godly lives.

One Sunday morning, after the service, this man approached me, dressed in his Royal Ranger uniform, and said, "Hello, my name is Commander Smith [not his real name], and I wanted to let you know I run Royal Rangers, and I'm responsible for all the young boys from the age of five to the age of sixteen in the church." Of course, it was not the best idea to inform the new senior pastor that you were "responsible" for all the boys. But he continued, "And as a result of running Royal Rangers, I want you to know that I'll be taking all these young men away multiple weekends to go camping, and we will not be in church on Sundays, but we'll be with all these young boys, anyone who we can get in our church from the age of five to the age of sixteen. And I just want you to know who I am and what we're doing."

In essence, this man believed that his vision for the young boys of the church was more important than the overall vision for the church. He did not understand the necessity of being willing to submit his vision to the restraints of the big picture.

And so I thanked him for introducing himself to me, and I replied, in an attempt to help him understand this principle, "I appreciate your heart for the young men. I think it might have been better for you to have said, 'Hello, Pastor Steve. My name is Commander Smith, and up until now I've been entrusted with the young men in the church from the age of five to sixteen, and I was wondering if you had a vision for Royal Rangers, and if so, what is that vision so I can know it and carry it? And would you like me to continue to serve as the commander, or would you like somebody else to do that? I was thinking maybe if you did want me to continue taking the young guys camping and missing church on multiple weekends, I was wondering how you would feel about that?'" I wanted to help him. I wanted to explain how his approach should be to submit to the big picture.

He simply replied, "That is not what I said," to which I responded, "I know that's not what you said, but it's what you should have said." After that exchange, he remained resolute in his position. He still perceived that the mission of the Royal Rangers should supersede the vision of the church.

He then said, "Well, I want a Scripture for why I should obey." Now, I have no problem with questions, and I am happy to discuss why I believe what I believe for our church. However, his demeanor and tone was one of disrespect, or suspicion, rather than humility. Then he said to me, "Well, how many weekends can we take the guys?"

And I said, "None. I don't want any young boy missing church on a Sunday morning because of something a church department is doing. We're not actually cutting our nose off to spite our face. We want to teach these young men to love God's house, not to be gone camping when church is in service!"

He would not relent. He said to me again, "I need a Scripture to explain why you're saying this. I can't understand why we can't have our campfire meetings."

And I said, "Well, when Mary lost Jesus at the age of twelve, a perfect candidate for Royal Rangers, she didn't find him at a Royal Rangers campfire. She found him in the house of God."[27] I went on to provide him with additional clear passages in the Bible that outline why the house of God should always have first priority.

The Bible instructs us to neglect not the gathering together of the saints as some have the habit of doing—we are not going to create habits for young boys to miss church and not to be in church by having a church department that takes them away from church.[28] If anything, we want to teach our young boys to be like Jesus, to be in the house of God every chance they get. And Jesus did say, "I will build my church"— and not Royal Rangers—"and the gates of hell will not prevail against it."[29]

Unfortunately, Commander Smith could not accept the vision that the church had for the young men. Had he been willing to submit, I would have been happy to find a compromise. We could have had the Royal Rangers continue, and they could have had the program, so long as they were in church on Sunday. There was no reason they couldn't camp on Friday night and all day Saturday and still return the boys to their families to be in church. I had attempted to ask Commander Smith to submit his vision to the restraints of the big picture so that we could continue to build God's house and he would find personal fulfillment in the midst of that. I'm saddened by his inability to change. He ended up leaving our church to pursue a church that would allow him to do what he wanted to do, rather than remain in a church that was going to lead with the vision of the senior pastor. He did not understand that following the vision and living within its restraints always includes submission to the big picture.

WITH THE RIGHT VISION, THE WORLD IS WON

The church is the hope of the world. I could never submit the vision of the church to a para-church ministry. There are many great causes and great organizations helping people in need all around the world. Royal Rangers does amazing things for thousands of boys. And yet, the church is the one place that God decreed would stand forever. The church is the one place charged to proclaim the good news of the gospel of Christ. The power of the vision of the house of God is that it wins the world.

Without the vision of God's house, the world would be perhaps as it was in Noah's day. Just before the flood, God expressed His disappointment with humanity. In Genesis 6:5 we read, "Then the Lord saw that the wickedness of man was great in the earth, and that every intent of the thoughts of his heart was only evil continually." The condition of man had reached a place where vision for anything good was gone. As a result, the people lived only for temporary, fleshly pleasures. They cast off restraint, and God destroyed all but one family as a result.

Fortunately, God made a way for man to avoid the fate suffered by the inhabitants of earth in Noah's day. He sent Jesus, who promised, "I have come that you might have life, and have it more abundantly."[30] Jesus gave us the greatest vision of all, the vision of a life poured out in saving others. He gave us a vision of eternal significance. When the church effectively lives out His vision, temporary, fleshly pleasures are easy to overcome. We restrain ourselves from the temptations of the world because we have a vision to win the world.

In building the church, I have discovered that the vision of Jesus to save the lost is fully realized when the leader of God's house uses the vision God has given him or her to challenge and encourage the people in the church. Over the years, I have come to understand the importance of vision casting. In fact, it is imperative that a leader constantly be sharing the vision that God has given him or her on a regular basis. At our church, we have Leadership Training Nights so that our people can come and hear the vision clearly and learn how to implement it so that the world can be won.

A leader knows when the vision has become fully internalized by the people when he or she hears it repeated back as it was originally stated. This takes time and consistency. There are three phases of comprehension that occur in vision casting.

PHASE 1: THE PEOPLE HEAR IT AND CAN REPEAT IT

This is the first level of communication. When the people repeat it, the vision is clear and is a mirror image of the leader's statements. However, at this stage, the people are merely connecting on a mental level, which means they are simply following directions and have yet to "own" the vision.

PHASE 2: THE PEOPLE BEGIN TO HAVE EMOTIONAL REACTIONS
TO HEARING IT REPEATEDLY

At this second and most crucial phase, the people begin to have a true heart response to the vision. At this stage, people begin to identify with the vision and wrestle with its meaning for their life on a heart level. Sometimes the reaction can seem negative because people are trying to process the deeper meanings of the vision. This can come in the form of people rolling their eyes, exclaiming, "Oh, no, not again!" Sometimes a person will ask the question, "How many times do I have to repeat this?" The answer is, obviously a lot more!

If the leader asks the question, "Are people ever going to get this vision?" The answer is yes; however, the leader must be willing to continue repeating himself. The law of repetition is powerful and over time, will lead to the discovery by the leader that the people are truly following the vision. As I've already mentioned, a key expression for our leadership team at Wave Church is: *don't blame people; train people.* Part of training is the repeated downloading of the vision of the senior leader.

PHASE 3: THE PEOPLE MAKE IT THEIR OWN BY LIVING IT OUT

This is the breakthrough phase. People proclaim the vision out of their own internal passions and personal revelations. Only then can a leader even begin to think she's scratched the surface of making sure people understand the vision. Only then will the effectiveness of the vision be strong enough that we can truly see the world won for Jesus.

RESTRAINTS OF THE VISION IN CHURCH LIFE

Our church has experienced tremendous growth in our young adult and youth ministries over the past ten years. We have been blessed to have many great leaders, both pastors and volunteers, who led the charge among the younger people. I believe this growth is a direct result of a key vision of our church. I have a vision to see young men and women grow up in the church in love with Jesus with their whole heart. I have a vision to see them love not only God, but also His house.

I have a great concern that too often in church by the time students graduate from children's ministry and into middle school, and even into high school youth ministry, many of them haven't spent a minute in the corporate church services. They've been marginalized and ministered to outside of the context a church service. They are dropped off by Mom and Dad at "kid's church" and are picked up after the main service is over. The effect of this is when a young person gets to an age where there's nothing left for them to do except go to church, they have not really been in church. They've been in children's ministry and Sunday school, but they've never been a part of the church. And then parents and leaders can't figure out why they don't want to go to church. I can tell them why—because we've never introduced them to the power of corporate worship and the love of God's house.

For our church, as I mentioned in the illustration earlier with the leader of the Royal Rangers, having our young people in church is a non-negotiable element of our vision. It is imperative to me that when we meet together on Sunday that the children are with us for the praise and worship. Some parents don't appreciate it, and some don't like it, because they want their kids out so they're not a distraction. I think the exact opposite. I think that by our worshipping God and having them with us that we're teaching the parents how to teach their kids how to behave in God's house; we're teaching them how to love God's house. We must bring our families into God's house. Joshua said, "As for me and my house, we will serve the Lord."[31] How will our children know how to serve the Lord if they have not been exposed to the full presence of God in His house?

We ask our parents to wear the restraints of this vision. We ask them to keep their children (over age four) in the service until the preaching of the Word so the kids can see adults in love with God, worshiping with all their hearts. Sometimes it's inconvenient. Sometimes it's challenging. Occasionally, a parent will have to take their child out because he or she is misbehaving. But, over time, there is no bigger key to developing a passionate group of young adults. We must include them, not quarantine them to a "kid's church" while the full manifestation of God's love and glory is revealed only to the adults.

I believe this is a vision not just for our church, but also for all churches. If you are reading this, and you are a senior pastor, I encourage you to implement this vision in your church. Ask your parents to wear the restraints of this vision, and don't be surprised when you begin to see great fruit in the lives of your young people over the course of time.

DEVELOP THE RESTRAINTS OF THE VISION

1. Do you listen to the call of your vision or the voices of those who say it can't be done? Have you written your vision down, clearly and in detail? If not, do so now!

2. Is your vision significant enough to overcome temporary distractions and temptations? Are there any areas of weakness in your life that cause you to stumble repeatedly? What is your vision for that area that will enable you to have the necessary restraints to overcome that weakness for good?

3. Is your vision submitted to the big picture? Are you able to remain patient and humble even when your ideas are not implemented?

4. Is your vision aligned with the mission of Christ? Are you winning the world? Are your people living with restraint, or is there a bigger vision needed to move them? Are your own insecurities preventing that bigger vision from being expressed?

FAVOR

Let not mercy and truth forsake thee: bind them about thy neck; write them upon the table of your heart: So shall you find favor and good understanding in the sight of God and man.

Proverbs 3:3-4

Today, the world exists in a season of God's favor, as proclaimed by Jesus himself. It is the will of God for us to live in favor with Him and with mankind. God's favor comes when we abide by His rules. In order to keep His favor, we must learn to "be good with good." The favor of God has a gathering spirit, helps us to understand the hearts of people, and give us opportunities to influence everyone around us for the purposes of God.

A cat won't curry favor even if it's in their best interests to do so. A cat can't be a hypocrite. If more preachers were like cats, this would be a more religious country.

—Stephen King

WE ARE LIVING IN THE YEAR OF THE LORD'S FAVOR, AS PROCLAIMED BY JESUS HIMSELF

Over the past thirty years in some Christian circles, the word *favor* has been improperly used. The concept of God's favor effecting and aiding our daily lives is a biblical one; however, it can be and has been warped by some preachers as a spiritual defense for a lust for material wealth. It has been preached that those who do not have earthly riches must somehow be outside the will of God. Favor is a legitimate expression of God's love toward his children, but it is not a license to pursue material possessions at the expense of loving our neighbor.

At the other end of the spectrum, there is a theology that has taught Christians for centuries that only a poor person can truly be holy and devout in their worship of God. This is just as dangerous and unbiblical as the teaching that *favor* means a Christian has done something wrong if she is not living in a mansion and driving a Bentley. The lack of material possessions does not make a person righteous, any more than an abundance of earthly wealth demonstrates that a person is "chosen" by God. Balance is critical in this area. It is not the money or possessions that demonstrate a person's alignment with God's will; it is her response to those things. The Bible clearly teaches the principle of God's favor, and I believe that it is a real, powerful, and essential part of a leader's life.

When Jesus shed his blood for all mankind, he made the favor of God available to all who believe in Jesus. He said to his disciples in John 10:15, "I have come that you might have life and you might have it more abundantly." The abundant life is characterized by God's favor. The importance of God's favor for the Christian is highlighted by the first recorded scripture that Jesus read in the synagogue. Jesus said in Luke 4:18-19, "The Spirit of the Lord is upon me, because He has anointed me to preach the gospel to the poor; He has sent me to heal the broken-hearted, to proclaim liberty to the captives and recovery of sight to the blind, to set at liberty those who are oppressed. To proclaim the year of the Lord's favor."

When Jesus read that passage from Isaiah, he was demonstrating to the people that He was the Messiah, and that by his coming death and resurrection, the favor of the Lord would be accessible to all who believed! Jesus said he was anointed to proclaim the year of the Lord's favor.

Jesus was strategic and bold when He declared that the Lord's favor was now. And yet, we are often embarrassed by God's favor in our lives. We're worried that others might think we are spending too much on a car or a home. I've said many times as pastor of my church, "I can never have a car poor enough for some people." This is my way of explaining that I will not allow an individual's perception of material blessings to control my enjoyment of God's favor.

We have got to be good with the good things in life. When a businessperson begins to experience God's blessings toward them and they get a new car or a new house, a promotion or opportunities to travel, I'll comment, "Hey, I really love your new car," and they'll almost apologize for it. I make sure to say, "Look, you need to be good with good. God has been good to you. It's the goodness of God. It's the glory of God to show his favor in your life." Remember, Jesus announced the season of God's favor when He read about His life fulfilling the prophecies of Isaiah, as recorded in Luke 4:19.

I'll often hear doomsday preachers talk about how various tragedies on earth are the judgment of God. I've heard preachers claim that September 11th was the judgment of God because the Church has failed to be all that she's called to be and because America has allowed homosexuality and abortion in the country. I've seen these church leaders declare that God is judging us by allowing madmen to fly planes into buildings, or by allowing natural disasters. I do not believe that that is the era in which we live. We are living in days of mercy and of grace; we are living in the year of God's favor.

Of course, there are consequences for sinfulness. As Romans 6:23 clearly explains, "For the wages of sin is death." I do believe in the judgment of God. I do believe we'll all go through the Bema Seat, also known as the Great White Throne of Judgment. There will be a final judgment at the end times.[32] I also believe that judgment starts first in the House of God.[33] All these things I believe, but I also understand that we live in a new covenant with a better hope and better promises.

At the cross, Jesus showed His love, mercy, grace, and His forgiveness and goodness toward mankind, and until He comes again, there is an opportunity for us to reach out to all people, regardless of their past or their sin, and to proclaim what Jesus proclaimed—this is the year of the Lord's favor!

When doomsday preachers condemn the world, I do not believe they are speaking out of a revelation of the New Testament and the new covenant in which we live. I used to hear someone prophesy for many years in New Zealand that the judgment of God is going to come against Auckland in an earthquake. He told us to fill our bathtubs with water, go to the supermarket, and fill our cupboards and pantries with food, because God is going to judge New Zealand.

To say that God is still judging the world in this manner is to say that Jesus' sacrifice on the cross was not good enough. 1 Peter 3:18 (NASB) states, "For Christ died for sins *once for all*, the just and the unjust, so that He might bring us to God, having been put to death in the flesh, but made alive in the spirit" (emphasis added).

Because of this verse, and many others, I disagree with the premise of the "condemnation and judgment" preachers—we are not living in that day of judgment.

As leaders, we must understand the seasons we are in, and this is the time when God is proclaiming favor and good news to the poor, to set at liberty those who are captive, to proclaim the good and the acceptable year of the Lord's favor.

IT IS GOD'S WILL FOR US TO LIVE IN FAVOR WITH GOD AND MAN

Another misguided perspective on God's favor is the notion that if a person sought and received the favor of God, he could not have favor with man. Most of the people who believe this fallacy base it on the admonition to believers, found in James 4:4, which warns that being a friend of the world is to be an enemy of God. The purpose of James's teaching in this passage is to encourage the reader to refrain from lusting after things of the world. He was writing to a group of believers who struggled with desires of the flesh at the expense of the pursuit of God. He was not writing to correct people who had a right relationship with God and were simply living in the world and engaging in commerce with unbelievers. He was trying to correct a real problem, not pronounce a doctrine of isolationism.

The idea that one could not have favor from God and man is easy to refute. In a passage regarding Jesus as a twelve-year-old (Luke 2:52), the Bible explains that Jesus grew "in favor with God and man." If Christ had favor with man and He is the Son of God, the redeemer of man, it's a fairly safe assumption that His followers should expect to also have favor with man. This favor is also mentioned in the Old Testament. The exact same phrase is used to describe Samuel in 1 Samuel 2:26. The favor of God and the favor of man are not mutually exclusive. In fact, they are connected. When God pours out His favor on your life, it extends to your relationships with people. It shows up in business dealings, in family dynamics, in workplace conversations.

Not only that, James is writing against loving the things of the world. He is not preaching against the possibility that people in the world might show you favor. I have absolutely no doubt it is the will of God for us to walk in His favor, and when we walk in the favor of God, we will receive the favor of man.

OBEYING GOD'S RULES RELEASES GOD'S FAVOR: RULE #1: GIVE GOD YOUR FIRST AND BEST

The example of Christ in Luke 2:52 is a straightforward description of a mature person following God's will and the natural growth that results. Beyond this perfect illustration found in the Gospels, the Old Testament is full of stories of men and women who lived in the favor of God. It also gives us a powerful example of a choice that did not earn God's favor, in the story of Cain and Abel.

> In the course of time Cain brought some of the fruits of the soil as an offering to the LORD. And Abel also brought an offering—fat portions from some of the firstborn of his flock. The LORD looked with favor on Abel and his offering, but on Cain and his offering He did not look with favor. So Cain was very angry, and his face was downcast. Then the LORD said to Cain, "Why are you angry? Why is your face downcast? If you do what is right, will you not

be accepted? But if you do not do what is right,
sin is crouching at your door; it desires to have
you, but you must rule over it."

Genesis 4:3-7

This passage explains the difference between the sacrifices of Cain and Abel, and how God responded by granting favor to Abel and withholding favor from Cain. Cain brought "some of the fruits," but Abel brought the "fat portions from…the firstborn." God was not upset with Cain because he brought fruit instead of animal sacrifice. God did not show favor toward Cain because Cain's sacrifice was not the first. One of the primary commandments, in fact, perhaps the pre-eminent law of God in the Old Testament, is to keep Him first. The story of Israel is the repeated failure of the people to keep Him first. God wants our first and best, to show Him that our hearts are fully His.

As the Lord looked at the respective offerings of Cain and Abel, He noticed Abel had given a sacrifice of the firstborn. Abel obeyed God's command to give God the first. God saw Cain was downcast and angry because of God's inability to show favor for disobedience. He instructs Cain to "do what is right and you will be accepted." He gave Cain the opportunity for repentance and obedience. Cain knew what God wanted, and he still chose to give God "some of the fruits" instead of the first of the fruits.

Notice how Cain's emotions were affected by his unwillingness to give up the first for God. The Bible says that Cain was downcast, which is translated from a Hebrew phrase that literally means his "face fell."

When we fail to obey God with our sacrifice, most commonly shown by our giving, our faces fall. We have a sour expression, a sad demeanor, because we realize that God is not showing us favor. And yet, like Cain, we either have too much pride or are too wrapped up in our possessions that we refuse to change. It's amazing how money can control and affect people's emotions. All we have to do to experience His favor is to give Him our first and best.

> How people found favor:
> Laban: favor by association
> Esther: favor by humility
> Nehemiah: favor by perseverance
> Noah: favor by righteousness

FAVOR CAN BE SHOWN BY GOD REGARDLESS OF EXTERNAL ECONOMIC CIRCUMSTANCES

I learned long ago never to allow money to rule my emotions. I could not lead others effectively if I let news reports about the economy determine my outlook. When the newspapers and television shows talk about the recession, I tell our congregation: "I've made a decision about the recession—I'm not joining it!" Some people are happy when they have lots of it, and some people are depressed when they have none. If you ride that emotional roller coaster where you allow the amount coming in and through your life to sway your emotions, you'll be ineffective; you'll be an upand-down Christian.

Paul said, in Philippians 4:11-13:

> I rejoiced greatly in the Lord that at last you renewed your concern for me. Indeed, you were concerned, but you had no opportunity to show it. I am not saying this because I am in need, for I have learned to be content whatever the circumstances. I know what it is to be in need, and I know what it is to have plenty. I have learned the secret of being content in any and every situation, whether well fed or hungry, whether living in plenty or in want. I can do all this through him who gives me strength.

This principle is essential for understanding that God's favor is not directly correlated the macro-economic environment. It does not matter if our business sector, our state, or even our nation is in financial decline. Whether we are well fed or hungry, whether in famine or in prosperity, whatever we do, we can trust in God's favor in our finances, regardless of the season.

The story of Joseph in the book of Genesis is a great example of someone who found favor from God in a time when his nation was in desperate straits. At each step along Joseph's journey, from the moment he was sold into slavery by his own brothers, Joseph received favor, in part because he kept the expectation of favor constant in his life.

Joseph found favor in the eyes of Potiphar and was placed in charge of his entire household. When Potiphar's wife attempted to seduce him, Joseph ran away and was falsely accused, which landed him in prison. He could have lamented his place and wondered if he had lost the favor of God, but he continued to believe, and soon, Joseph found favor in the eyes of the prison warden. The prison warden put him in charge of the other prisoners! Talk about favor! Sometimes in life we may find ourselves in a season that seems limiting or restricting, and sometimes through no fault of our own. May we take a lesson from Joseph and stay in faith and find ourselves, like him, ruling over the limitations.

Joseph's commitment to excellence regardless of circumstances eventually provided him an audience with the Pharaoh. When Pharaoh could not solve a troubling dream, Joseph was summoned because the butler remembered Joseph's discernment from his time in prison. As Pharaoh sought an explanation for the dream, Joseph was able to interpret Pharaoh's dream of the seven years of prosperity followed by the seven years of famine. While God gave Joseph the answer for Pharaoh, God was also teaching Joseph that regardless of the season, famine, or prosperity, you can believe in God's favor. Whatever the season, whether in famine or prosperity, God can show his favor to us. And most of the time, his favor arrives in unexpected ways. For example, the prophet Elisha thought he was going to die in a famine, but God used a raven to bring him food! Do not allow the current reality of the natural environment to diminish your expectation for God's favor. Never let the lack of finances control your spirit. Never let the abundance of finances cause you to forget God. Trust Him; believe that He wants to and will show you His favor.

UNTIL YOU BECOME GOOD WITH GOOD, YOU WILL NEVER FULLY EMBRACE GOD'S FAVOR

The Bible says that God is good, and what He does is good.[34] *Christianity is not a lifestyle enhancement program.* It is more than a set of rules for being blessed. It is full and complete surrender to the lordship of Jesus Christ. I certainly understand that outside of Jesus we are all lost, no matter how good or bad we think we are or have been. We should come to Christ not just so our life can get better, but so we actually learn how to be better. The Bible says there is none good save God alone, and we are all in desperate need of a Savior. The only way to God is through Jesus, and we must lose our life that we might find it.[35] I certainly believe that with all my heart. I believe that Jesus is the only way to the Father; faith in Christ is an internal redemption, not an outward cosmetic improvement process.

A person will never reach his full potential until he learns to be good with good. It's not just about going to heaven; it's about having the ability to resource the kingdom of God to reach the lost. And if we are not comfortable with success, with prosperity, or with favor in our lives, we will not be able to resource God's church to rescue those who don't yet know Jesus. Believe God for favor in your business decisions, and believe God for favor in your financial planning, so that His blessings will expand your ability to provide financially for pastors, for missions, for community care programs that reach the millions of people who are desperate for hope that can only be found in Jesus.

Favor isn't fair. Favor gives you an edge. We need to believe God for favor in our community; we need to believe God for favor in our jobs, with our bosses. We need to believe God for favor with our clients and our work, favor in our marriage, favor in our relationships, favor with the media, favor with politics, favor in every area of our lives. Psalm 23:6 says, "Surely goodness and mercy will follow me all the days of my life."

I often picture those characteristics of God like two little puppy dogs named goodness and mercy. I believe that they are following me. I believe that when we learn to walk in the favor of God, we get good with good. We receive the favor and are open to a greater opportunity to give to the vision and mission of the local church.

I remember when I married Sharon in 1983 and we were on our honeymoon. I was overwhelmed with everything that had taken place. In three short years, I had turned from a path of self-destruction to a road of unbelievable blessing. I had become a Christian and surrendered my life to become a preacher of the gospel. I met a beautiful girl, who was in love with God and me, and I had gotten married. And I just remember thinking, "God, I hope I can live up to all of this." I felt an overwhelming sense of pressure and responsibility, because I didn't want to blow it. Most of my experience in family life had been dysfunction. I didn't know how to feel comfortable around normal people like my wife. She was a good person with great character and morals, even before she met Jesus. I was the complete opposite.

Everything in my life that was ever good somehow turned out to be ruined. I would make promises to my parents that I was going to start life all over again and live right. Those promises were broken within a week. If ever I got my hopes up, I knew I'd just be hurt and disappointed again, so I'd stopped trying. And then I met Jesus, which was the greatest day of my life. Then, on the second greatest day of my life, here I'm married, I'm twenty years old, the goodness of God's favor is evident in my life, and I was too afraid to accept it all, because I was not able to be good with good.

I kept thinking, *I've got this beautiful girl who's dedicated her life to be married to me, and I have this overwhelming sense of responsibility, this sense of is this too good to be true.* I was so afraid that I would do something to destroy everything. These thoughts were racing through my mind during our honeymoon. And then the most amazing experience happened.

God spoke to me in an audible voice while we were on our honeymoon! The only time I can honestly say that God spoke to me and I heard him speak audibly was when he spoke to me about Sharon. She was sleeping, and I was tossing and turning, when God said, "This is a very special young woman I've given to you, and I want you to love her as I do the Church." I was overwhelmed. I was stunned. His voice was as the Bible describes, like the sound of rushing waters and thunder. It was majestic, and I was in absolute awe (and a little scared) in that moment.

I remember sitting in the hotel room just feeling overwhelmed that God cared and understood all my feelings of inadequacy and insecurity. I wasn't good with good, and I was struggling with accepting all the goodness that He had brought into my life—this beautiful girl, our vision for the future, and His calling to ministry. But God understood all my fears. He knew my concerns and spoke to me. He showed me His favor.

As I sat there half-smiling and half-trembling, Sharon woke up. I did not tell her anything, but she knew something significant had happened. She looked at me, and she burst into tears and said, "God is in this room." She still sensed the remnants of the presence of God and His voice without me telling her what happened.

I said, "You have no idea how much God was in this room." And I told her what God spoke to me about her, and she just smiled and said, "I like God." That was the beginning of God teaching me to be good with good.

God wants you to be in a good church. I've heard people say, "Every church I've ever been to I've been hurt." That comment comes from someone who has not learned to be good with good. I've heard women say, "Every relationship I've ever had, every guy I've ever dated has been a loser." I often, kindly but directly, explain to those ladies, "If you keep turning up at the scene of the accident, there's one common denominator—*you*." I realize, of course, that many bad things happen to good people, and there are plenty of bad guys who do horrible things to nice women. But if it's a perpetual situation, maybe there is an opportunity for her to examine her own expectations and attitudes and perhaps discover areas that are preventing her from experiencing the favor of God in relationships.

Could it really be that every church you've attended was evil? Every person you've ever dated, every boss you've ever had, and every pastor you've ever trusted is a worthless, horrible person? Sometimes we think if we can just get away from where we are and move somewhere else then life will be better. There's only problem with that notion: wherever *you go*, there *you are*. And if you have not learned to be good with good, you will end up attracting bad situations. Until you learn to be good with good, you cannot embrace the goodness of God and what He has for you.

It is essential that we develop the ability to break through our personal hang-ups and weaknesses. We must overcome those little thoughts that mock us, that tell us we don't deserve nice things, that the goodness and mercy of God are only for the "good" people. When we can't get past those insecurities, we end up like Shakespeare's Macbeth, unfit for the title and position of king.

Angus, one of the characters in *Macbeth*, paints a powerful word picture of this principle. He describes Macbeth's title of king as ill-fitting, something that hangs on him loosely, "like a giant's robe / upon a dwarfish thief." That expression is a perfect illustration of how we feel and behave if we don't understand that God's favor is real and we are heirs with Christ. We must become good with good so that His favor "fits" us like a custom-tailored suit, and not a "giants robe… upon a dwarfish thief."

THE FAVOR OF GOD OPERATES AS A GATHERING SPIRIT; IT HELPS YOU UNDERSTAND PEOPLE'S HEARTS

Often people in our local area say, "Steve, before you walked into our store, nobody was here, but after you walked in here, people came into the store. You're good for business." At first I laughed it off. But as time passed, and more people commented on it at a variety of shops, I noticed it was true!

I believe this is an example of walking in God's favor. His favor works as a gathering spirit; it is always open for more people to be influenced and blessed. When we walk in God's favor, we bring His blessing. In the Old Testament story of Jacob and his father-in-law, we see an example of the favor of God spreading blessing to people who are simply near the man or woman receiving favor. Laban, who made Jacob work a total of fourteen years to marry his daughter Rachel, told Jacob that the Lord had favored him and blessed him because of Jacob."[36] It's important to be careful where we bring that blessing and that favor. When you carry the favor of God, people who don't know you very well will open up to you and confide in you. They will say, "I don't know why I'm telling you this, but I feel like I can trust you." That's the favor of God. It gives you opportunities to be a blessing, but it also carries a responsibility to handle it with care, because people will be drawn to you, and their hearts will be open to your voice.

The favor of God opens doors for you where doors would not naturally be opened. The favor of God will close doors for you that need to be closed. The favor of God will give you divine connections with people that you could not have otherwise met but for His favor. The principle of God's favor is something that we need to pray for. It's something we need to access. It's something that we need to understand.

The favor of God carries a gathering mentality. Jesus walked in this daily. In one example, after the Pharisees saw all the sinners drawn to Him, they complained about the type of people and the size of the crowds that Jesus gathered. He then told them the parable of the man with one hundred sheep, who, after losing one, left the ninety-nine and searched for the lost one until he found it.[37] This is the attitude that comes with God's favor. There is always one more to be found, to be included in what God has planned for this world. When we believe God for His favor, it brings favor to reach people.

Reaching people is great, but connecting with people and drawing them to Jesus requires an understanding of the human heart.

In John 2:24-25, the Bible states, "But Jesus would not entrust himself to them, for he knew all people. He did not need any testimony about mankind for He knew what was in each person." He knew everything there was to know about man. Joseph had to instruct Jesus in carpentry. Mary might have instructed Him in reading or writing. But Jesus did not need instruction for insight into the hearts of man. He certainly learned the Scriptures and was regularly dedicated to the temple and reading Scripture.

But no one needed to teach Him anything about people. The passage above says he needed no testimony about man. He knew everything there was to know about man. The favor of God provided Jesus with amazing people skills. People were drawn to Him because the favor of God gave Him an understanding and empathy for the deep, hidden parts of the human heart.

Unfortunately, many Christians approach people to talk about Jesus and the response is elbows and heels. I see some street preachers down on the oceanfront here in Virginia Beach, and while I know they mean well, they are preaching a turnorburn Christianity with the entire emphasis on the fact that people without Christ are going to hell. There is a hell. I do not dispute its existence or the need for people to accept Jesus as their Savior or they will enter hell after this life.[38] I do agree that everyone must have a lifechanging encounter with Jesus, and everyone must enter into a relationship with Jesus as a result of awareness of our own sins and our need for a Savior. However, as Christians, we need to believe God for the wisdom to proclaim this message, which is good news. The gospel is the preaching of good news to the poor, to proclaim the year of the Lord's favor. Tragically, all some Christians see are people running the other direction because they are focusing on punishment rather than the overwhelming love of Christ.

Jesus was able to draw people near rather than drive them away because he understood the human heart. He recognized that the power of love is far greater than the threat of punishment. He knew this through God's favor, for it gave him the ability to understand the heart of man. When we seek and accept God's favor, it only improves our capacity for reaching others, because it expands our capacity for knowing the human heart.

Jesus knew from the beginning who would betray Him.[39] This is because he understood the hearts of men. How great a leadership skill is that? I pray for more of that gift—to have more of God's favor to understand the hearts of men and operate with the gathering spirit. I'll often sit in a coffee shop for hours and just stare at people and watch them and smile, looking at them as I think God might be looking at them. He delights in the diversity of people and the variety of their spirits. My friend Phil Baker often says, "If people were a painting, they'd be a Picasso. If people were cars, they'd be Rolls Royces. If they were watches, they'd be Rolexes."

People are extraordinary, and when we view them this way, it's easy to access God's favor, because we operate with the gathering mentality of the man looking for his lost sheep. I've experienced this in abundance on occasions in my life.

I was actually in a coffee shop one morning, reading the passage in Luke 15 that tells the story of the lost sheep. As I was sitting there, a woman walked up to me and said, "Excuse me, I don't know you, but I believe you can help me, could I please talk to you?" I looked up at this woman, and I could see her spirit—quietly clamoring for a connection with something deeper. My pastor's heart was moved to encourage her. I asked her to sit down, although I was waiting for a pastor to join me for an appointment. She started to pour out her heart, sharing her life story—the challenges she'd faced in life and how she felt very alone, almost friendless. I told her about our church and our women's ministry and how I believed there was a place for her to fit in and find friendship in our small groups. She was very encouraged by it all, and she left with an elevated spirit.

As I was talking to that woman, the lady sitting next to us heard me talking and said to me after the woman left, "Excuse me, I heard you talking with that woman, and I've got some challenges with my children. Could I talk to you?" We talked for a few minutes, and I told her about our children's department at church and our children's pastors and encouraged her to come visit our services. I was able to encourage her that she didn't have to try to raise the kids without support and that there were plenty of opportunities for her to get together with other moms and find encouragement and strength.

As I was talking to her about that, a hairdresser walked in and heard me talking to this lady, and after she left, she said, "Excuse me, I heard you talking to that lady. Could I please talk to you?"

And I laughed and said, "Sure. Take a seat." The pastor who was waiting to meet with me had arrived and now had to sit and wait as I talked to all these people. When the hairdresser left, I said to the pastor, "Come on, let's go somewhere else so we can actually have a moment by ourselves. This is incredible what's been happening."

And so we went to an Applebee',s trying to get away from where we were, and we're both laughing about the stream of people who had approached me in the coffee shop. We sat down at the restaurant, and I started telling him about this prayer that I'm praying for the favor of God and how God is just suddenly bringing people to me as I'm asking God to give me that gathering mentality. I was asking God to give me that desire. I wanted to be like the shepherd seeking his lost sheep; I wanted to understand the hearts of people.

And as I'm telling that story to this pastor, a perfect stranger walks up to me, a businessman, and hands me his business card, which identified him as the president of a technology company. He said, "I don't know you, but I believe you can help me. I'm in trouble. Please call me on this number," and then he walked out of Applebee's.

My head was spinning. I'm thinking, *God, what is all this about?*

And I felt like the Lord said, "You wanted to know everything to know about people. This is how much need is out there."

The favor of God is a people magnet. I didn't ask for those people to approach me, but they did because they were drawn by the favor of God. That experience demonstrates the gathering spirit that comes from God's favor. When you really tap into the heart of God, His favor sends a gathering mentality. When you access the favor of God, you gain the ability to understand the hearts of people. Through His favor, God will bring you opportunities to help others, because He fills you with a heart that reaches out to and cares for people. People sense that, and they are drawn to the favor of God in you.

THE FAVOR OF GOD IN CHURCH LIFE

I am absolutely convinced that I have been favored by God to reach the lost. I was born to make heaven throw a party. Luke 15:10 reads, "There is joy in the presence of the angels over one sinner who repents." I like making the angels joyful. By God's grace, in our church we regularly see over one hundred people every week make decisions for Jesus, and we see many, many people come into the kingdom of God.

Because you attract what you respect, our church is a people magnet. We respect all people and desire that all would come to know Him. We talk about an attitude of being a "bringer" not an "inviter." Our people bring their friends to church with a passion to see them meet Christ. In fact, during our altar calls, I routinely ask people to turn to their friends and offer to walk forward with them so there are no hindrances of shame or fear to keep the lost and broken from meeting Christ.

I am grateful to God that someone brought me to church. My good friend Gerard Keehan brought me to church as a seventeen-year-old. Though I was a teenager, I was already an alcohol-drinking, fighting, partying, wild man. Gerard brought me, and he would not let me go. He had the gathering mentality that comes with the favor of God. When we have that favor, we have to reach out to people and bring them to Christ.

One of the intentional ways that we see God's favor in our church is in our connection to the military. As I've mentioned, we are located in a significant military area, and we highly respect our armed forces. We pray for God's favor with the military, and I proclaim it regularly before our congregation. During our prayer request and praise report moments in church, we almost always give thanks for our military. When we appreciate our military in service, our people never fail to give them a standing ovation.

Through the favor we've had with the military, God has opened amazing doors for us to influence the armed services. I've had the incredible privilege to twice be on an aircraft carrier. We send care packages with DVDs and CDs of our church services to military installations around the world. People frequently ask me how we were able to get such a large number of Navy SEALs and Special Operations personnel in our church. It's simple: I believe in the favor of God with the military. As a result we now have over four hundred active military families in our church! Whatever you respect, you attract. Seek God's favor for people in your community. Respect them, accept them, and watch God's favor bring them in.

SEEK AND ACCEPT THE FAVOR OF GOD

1. Do you genuinely believe that we live in a period of an outpouring of God's favor? If not, why not? If so, are you daily believing for and walking in His favor?

2. Do you follow rule number one? Do you give God your first and best? How is your tithing? Remember,

the tithe belongs to God; it was never yours. What are you sacrificing to honor and worship God? How are you seeking His favor by serving Him?

3. Do you struggle with being good with good? When was the last time you went somewhere that was so nice or upscale that you felt uncomfortable? Place yourself in an environment that is "above" you on a regular basis. This will enable you to more quickly become good with good.

4. Do you have a gathering mentality? Are you a people magnet? Do you look for opportunities to include others? Do you actively seek out new relationships so that you may continue to see God's favor expanding your world?

THE HOLY SPIRIT

But you shall receive power, after that the Holy Spirit is come upon you: and you shall be witnesses unto me both in Jerusalem, and in all Judaea, and in Samaria, and unto the uttermost part of the earth.

Acts 1:8

The Holy Spirit is God's voice to the church today. God, through the Holy Spirit, has a unique message to bring to your church. Signs and wonders follow the preaching of the gospel; they are not independent from the good news of Jesus. The Holy Spirit never wants to offend unbelievers, and the Holy Spirit is always relevant to contemporary culture.

Wise leaders should have known that the human heart can not exist in a vacuum…Christ died for our hearts and the Holy Spirit wants to come and satisfy them.

—A.W. Tozer

Holy Spirit filled souls are ablaze for God. They love with a love that glows. They serve with a faith that kindles. They serve with a devotion that consumes. They hate sin with fierceness that burns. They rejoice with a joy that radiates.

—Samuel Chadwick

GOD HAS A UNIQUE MESSAGE FOR YOUR CHURCH

IN the opening chapters of the book of Revelation, John records, through inspiration of the Holy Spirit, seven letters to seven different churches. Every church received a specific message. Whether it was a call to repent or a warning of coming hardship, the Spirit of the Lord moved through John to deliver a timely word that was unique to each circumstance.

1. Ephesus (Revelation 2:1-7): the church that had forsaken its first love.
2. Smyrna (Revelation 2:8-11): the church that would suffer persecution.
3. Pergamum (Revelation 2:12-17): the church that needed to repent.
4. Thyatira (Revelation 2:18-29): the church that had a false prophetess.
5. Sardis (Revelation 3:1-6): the church that had fallen asleep.
6. Philadelphia (Revelation 3:7-13): the church that had endured patiently.
7. Laodicea (Revelation 3:14-22): the church with the lukewarm faith.

I believe that God, through the Holy Spirit, is speaking to our churches today. Each one has a unique mission within the collective call to rescue the lost and baptize and make disciples. Whether it's our busy modern lifestyle or an emphasis on other elements of worship, I believe the church has neglected to wait and listen for the Holy Spirit. In order to discover what he wants to say to our local church where we lead and serve, we must make time to listen for Him. I often tell my church that the Holy Spirit is a gentleman—He will never force you into anything. He is patient and waiting for you to seek Him and to listen for His voice. He descended on Jesus at His baptism like a dove, an international symbol of peace and tranquility.[40]

He is speaking. Are our churches listening? Once we choose to listen, we must be content with His message for our church. He may challenge us, convict us, or encourage us to do more, try harder, or to repent. We must answer the challenge and follow the direction of the Holy Spirit. We must be submitted to the vision He is speaking to our local church.

Throughout my ministry, as I travel around the world and speak at many great churches, I witness a "Grass is Greener" phenomenon among believers. We hear about a move of the Spirit at another church or in another city, and we want that in our church, rather than what God wants in our church. This is a tragic mistake. Each church has a mandate from God for its city and its region. When the people of a church begin to desire the outward signs of the Holy Spirit from another place, they are basically telling God, "We don't want what you want for us. We want what those people over there are getting from you!"

This kind of attitude is not new. Remember the Israelites' journey in the wilderness for forty years? After God rescued them out of slavery in Egypt, and miraculously provided manna and quail every day, they complained because they wanted something different.

They even asked Moses to take them back to Egypt where they could eat the garlic, onions, and leeks that they were fed as slaves![41]

God designed the manna specifically to bless the Israelites. God has designed a specific word for your church. What He is saying to your church may not be (and probably isn't) what He wants your church to hear and do. And just because God is moving in a certain way at another place and God is speaking to a church about a specific issue doesn't necessarily mean that God is saying that to the entire body of Christ. I do believe there are certain emphases that every church ought to have—the emphasis of worship, the emphasis of giving, the emphasis of soul winning, and the emphasis of community outreach. I believe those key elements of service should be in every church, but how that is expressed can be as different and as unique as the personalities, backgrounds, and callings of the senior pastors and leaders at each church.

In the book of Revelation, the Spirit gave seven different messages to seven different churches. We can only effectively respond to His message for our local church. Make no mistake: God truly does have a unique message for your church.

SIGNS AND WONDERS FOLLOW THE PREACHING OF GOD'S WORD. WE DON'T CHASE SIGNS AND WONDERS.

Just as God is not pleased when we seek His message for another church as our own, it offends the Holy Spirit when we chase signs and wonders for their own sake. Seeking the miraculous is not wrong when you are desperate for God to work good in a situation that only He can rescue. But church hopping and traveling around to revival meetings or Christian conferences hoping to see a physical demonstration of God's power is dangerous and foolish. In fact, Jesus told the Pharisees that it is a "wicked and adulterous generation that seeks after signs."[42] He was warning them (and everyone who would read His words) against looking for signs to confirm that He is who He says He is. This behavior demonstrates a lack of faith, and without faith it is impossible to please God.[43]

Yet, Jesus' ministry was filled with miracles. John said that the world couldn't hold all the books that would be required to write down all the incredible wonders Jesus worked during his time on earth![44] Is Jesus contradicting His message to the Pharisees with His actions? Of course not. The reality is God's power is immeasurable, and His every interaction with humanity is miraculous. At His Word, the world was created. And when His word is preached, creative miracles happen! While it is true that Jesus warned us not to pursue signs and wonders, He told His disciples that the miraculous accompanies those who believe and preach the gospel.[45]

I remember a Sunday some years ago when somebody came running up to me after a service. They were so excited to speak to me. They explained that they were in a service at another church when gold dust began falling out of the ceiling, and people's teeth were miraculously filled with gold. The person telling me about this then asked why this wasn't happening in our church. I explained that while God can do anything, and what they saw may have been an actual miracle, our church is not seeking the unusual and bizarre in order to strengthen our faith in God.

There is only one thing we chase in our church. We are chasing the lost. We are rescuing desperate people and restoring broken families through the power of the gospel of Jesus Christ. We are raising leaders to multiply the message of hope to the world. We are not seeking gold dust from the sky. Maybe God did send gold into people's teeth; maybe that's His message for that particular church. We are listening, and we believe we know what God is saying to our church. We are open to the fullness of the Holy Spirit, and we want all that God has for us, but we do not chase signs and wonders. We preach the gospel, we believe in Jesus, and we know that signs and wonders will follow. *Far too often, Christians forget that the greatest miracle of all is salvation.* For our church, seeing dozens of people saved every weekend is the greatest sign and wonder of all.

I worry that our "Spirit-filled" churches are sometimes conditioning people to act with learned behavior in response to a style of prayer or a prophetic word. We have to be cautious that we don't allow the move of the Holy Spirit to become a routine part of the service where the same ten people fall down under the power of the Spirit every service or the same two people speak a word of prophesy every third Sunday. God is constant, but God is ever changing. He is pro-active, not reactive. When God is moving, we've got to move where God is moving.

There's a great line from an old Christian rock song "Beyond Belief" by the band Petra. It says, "We're content to pitch our tent, when the glory's evident. Seldom do we know the glory came and went." Too often, our people remain in the same atmosphere and the same activities because God once moved. Now God has moved on and been moved on for five to ten years, and our people remain in the past, recycling old works of God.

There have been phenomenal works of God and amazing movements birthed by His Spirit during the course of human history. He's taught us through many different great movements: the Protestant Reformation with its emphasis on salvation by grace through faith in Christ alone; Azusa Street and its emphasis on the baptism of the Holy Spirit, to name just two. We read about and are inspired by great speakers and healers like Charles G. Finney, Dwight L. Moody, and Smith Wigglesworth. In all of these examples, God poured out His Spirit on people through powerful movements. But we don't camp in any of those truths or movements. The Bible explains that a river of truth flows out of God.[46] Every move of God flows through that river and brings a tremendous truth. But a river moves on: it's never in one place; it's always surging forward. Trying to go back to a move of God is like trying to swim upstream. God wants to do something new, but those who want to linger in the past will find it unsettling, because they are actually resisting the next move of God.

Jesus taught how to respond to a move of God during the Mount of Transfiguration experience.

This miraculous event is recorded in the Gospels of Matthew, Mark, and Luke.

Peter, James, and John joined Jesus on a mountain. During their time, several figures appeared, which resembled Elijah and Moses. When Peter, the daring one, suggested they build a memorial to the moment, a cloud surrounded them and the audible voice of God was heard. They were terrified!

From the midst of the cloud, God said, "This is my Son, My Chosen; listen to him!"[47] When the cloud blew away, Moses and Elijah were gone, and Peter realized that he was better off keeping his mouth shut. He exhibited a common desire when something transcendent occurs in life with God. He wanted to make a tangible reminder of the event. But God told him to be quiet. And the disciples didn't mention the Transfiguration. You see, it wasn't about the event; it was about the change that happened in the event. Jesus was transfigured. He communicated with Moses and Elijah. They discussed His mission on earth. I like to think they encouraged Jesus. They gave Him support for what He was about to endure. Likewise, when we experience a "God moment," we must be careful to not emphasize the encounter. We must emphasize the work we are called to do as a result of the encounter.

The Christian leader should always stay in the Word of God and allow what God is doing today to be added to the truth. Even the great ministries mentioned above diminished or evolved as God moved on. God does not sit still. His signs and wonders always follow His Word, but if you try to chase the past, or chase His message for another place, you will end up out of sync and become incapable of effective leadership.

THE GIFTS OF THE HOLY SPIRIT SHOULD NOT OFFEND UNBELIEVERS

As mentioned earlier in this chapter, the Holy Spirit is a gentleman. His presence is described as a dove. He is gentle yet strong. He is dignified. And yet, at the day of Pentecost, the Holy Spirit appeared as flames of fire.[48] Jesus promised His disciples that He would send a Comforter who would bring power to their lives. *49* Like God, the Holy Spirit has multiple facets. Each aspect of His presence is real and important, yet how He is presented to unbelievers could either bring conversion or create a mass rush for the exits!

The apostle Paul takes several chapters in 1 Corinthians to discuss the works of the Holy Spirit. In particular, he uses 1 Corinthians 14 to outline the manifestations of the gifts of the Spirit in a church service. Many great books have been written on this subject, and I don't intend to attempt to bring a new revelation. It is my desire that this chapter reinforce the truth that Paul exhorts the church in Corinth: that all things should be done decently and in order.[50] God is speaking to men and women, encouraging them through the Spirit to come to Jesus. But, like Elijah experienced when he searched for God in a mighty wind, an earthquake, and a fire without finding Him, it's often not by demonstrations of power but by a "still, small voice."[51]

Sometimes people ask, "Is your church Spirit-filled?" because they're so used to the way things have been done in other churches where they're always looking for the supernatural by sensational things that are happening rather than allowing the supernatural to be simply super natural. The operation of the Holy Spirit is alive and well in our church, but it's not expressed in a mystical way. When I am sharing a word of knowledge or a prophetic word, I don't do it in a way that draws attention to myself and makes it spooky. I don't speak in the King James vernacular. I try to do it in a very natural, real way that people can understand. Because I believe the Holy Spirit is a gentleman and His gifts are expressed to unbelievers in a receivable fashion.

I absolutely believe in the gifts of the Holy Spirit, and I completely believe they are alive and well today. I have seen in my own life a young boy who drowned in a pool come back to life. I've seen somebody healed of HIV. I've seen angels play guitars in meetings. I've heard the audible voice of God. I've been to Papua New Guinea and seen a thousand people fall under the power of God. I've seen people experience the blessing of the Holy Spirit with joy and laughter. And yet, I always remember Paul's reminder that "God is not the author of confusion, but of peace."[52] God does things with order so as not to offend unbelievers, but to draw all men to repentance.

Some of you reading this will recognize moments in your life when you wanted to invite people to church but you didn't out of fear that something crazy might happen because you attended (or still attend) a church where the service is not done in order. Some of you were brave enough to invite them anyway, and you spent the entire service silently praying that no one felt led by the Spirit to start running around the room, or that "Sister Sally" didn't start speaking in tongues for ten minutes, and no one arose to provide the interpretation. As Paul repeatedly advised in 1 Corinthians, order and structure is the responsibility of the leaders and is necessary for the lost to be saved. An absence of structure to a service brings confusion, and it brings a cringe factor to a service that makes us reluctant to invite the unsaved.

If you are currently in a church that does not have order, or if you are leading a church that is confusing and chaotic, please re-evaluate your priorities. Enter a service and watch as though you knew nothing of the things of God or His Spirit. Would you want to stay? Would you ever return? If your answer to those questions is no, then now is the time to make changes. We have to remove the cringe factor from our churches if we ever expect to see souls saved.

We've got to look at all the things that make people cringe. God's vision is unique for each church, but He wants the Church to be relevant to its community. The house of God should be built upon the vision to reach out to the people in a manner that makes them desire to hear more. As pastors and leaders, you must be working to ensure that your church is the kind of church that would make people excited to bring their friends. There should be passionate praise and worship, clear and powerful preaching compelling people to give their life to Christ. We should remain open to the gifts of the spirit, but not in a flaky way. We should regularly review 1 Corinthians 14 as a model for the use of the gifts of the Spirit in church services. The Holy Spirit loves to draw people to Christ, and the gifts of the Holy Spirit should not offend unbelievers.

THE HOLY SPIRIT RELATES TO CULTURE

When we send missionaries to Africa, we teach them to adapt to the culture. We have courses in international business that teach crosscultural sensitivities to make sure that we don't offend people. We try to adapt to their culture. Well, why don't we do that in our churches right where we are? Why don't we understand the culture we're trying to reach? I've heard church leaders say, "Well, this is who we are. We do praise and worship like this. We have three hour services." There's nothing inherently wrong with the style or the length of the service, but it demonstrates a failure to recognize the culture. It shows a lack of appreciation for a different culture. Just as a person tries to learn the customs of a foreign land so as to avoid offenses, so we must learn the culture of the unsaved so that we can lead them to the cross without losing them before we get there.

The book of Acts explains that the Holy Spirit fell upon the disciples in the upper room, and they spilled out onto the streets speaking in other tongues. There were Jewish believers from all over the world: "Parthians and Medes and Elamites, those dwelling in Mesopotamia, Judea and Cappadocia, Pontus and

Asia, Phrygia and Pamphylia, Egypt and the parts of Libya adjoining Cyrene, visitors from Rome, both Jews and proselytes, Cretans and Arabs."[53] Everyone in the crowd all spoke different languages, and yet they exclaimed, "How is it we hear them speaking in our own language the praises of God?" Just like the apostles miraculously spoke and everyone heard the words in his own language, one of the evidences of being filled with the Spirit is the ability to speak the language of the culture and the community you are trying to reach.

Our church firmly believes relating to our culture without compromising the truth is a work of the Holy Spirit. We have many activities that are not "typical church," and yet we've seen thousands of people moved to follow Christ because they were introduced to the gospel in a welcoming, familiar environment.

For example, every Christmas we have Santa Claus show up for church. We've had him arrive as a Navy SEAL skydiving out of a helicopter. We've had him arrive on a Segway. He's shown up driving a fire engine. He's led a parade of Harley-Davidsons into the church parking lot. And after his grand entrance, the children gather around and he tells them the story of Jesus!

One of my all-time favorite moments in church happened on one of these nights. A great volunteer leader in our church dressed up as Santa Claus. The plan was for him to rappel from our catwalk (which is about the same height as the ceiling of Wave Convention Center). All the kids were gathered on stage, excitedly looking up as the jolly man in the red suit and fake beard began sliding down the ropes.

Unfortunately, about two-thirds of the way down, his fake beard got tangled in the rope. Santa hung there, twisting and turning. Each attempt to untangle the beard only got it more tied up. Finally, Santa abandoned the beard and slid to the ground. As he landed, his own four-year-old son shouted out, "Dad, you're a fake!" It was a priceless, hilarious moment. It was a family moment. I'm so glad we have that memory as a church.

We have a huge Halloween outreach. We bring in bounce houses and carnival-style games, and the kids run around in costumes and just have fun. Unfortunately, some overly religious Christians don't embrace these activities. They've told me that God couldn't possibly bless an event that's connected to something as evil as Halloween. The reality is God has blessed it. He's used it in a tremendous way. We've seen families saved who are now growing in Christ and leading in our church as a result of our Halloween outreach. I've had parents tell me they would have never come to church except for that Halloween night. And because of the hospitality and love and joy that they saw in our church that night, they came back. And they kept coming back and are now planted in the house of God.

And we teach people when we host a Halloween event not to think that we're compromising the gospel by giving people a positive alternative to reach out—to have somewhere to go on a night where parents are concerned for their children. But we create a great festival, a safe and a wholesome environment, a fun carnival for parents to bring their kids.

Now, some people get upset about that style of evangelism. We don't crucify Santa in our church. We don't beat up on the bunny at Easter. We don't hate Halloween. We don't curse the darkness. We light a candle. We use a variety of different, culturally relevant opportunities to reach the lost. We have a great Super Bowl night service. We reach out to people who wouldn't normally go to a church on that weekend because of the Super Bowl, so we show the Super Bowl on our big screens in our church.

We've been criticized. I've been told that our church is getting worldly. If Santa Claus and the Easter bunny and the Super Bowl are too worldly for some people, they should probably not bother coming around, because we are going to get even more "worldly," by their definition. We are going to reach our culture without compromise every chance we can. We are going to speak their language and understand their customs without diminishing the truth of Jesus Christ.

I remember at one community event our praise and worship team was performing country western music, and a newer person who had just come into our church was very offended. She said, "I can't stand this music. It's of the devil."

And I said, "I couldn't agree more." Then I smiled a bit and continued, "But it's not for us. It's for them," as I pointed to the hundreds of un-churched people in the parking lot.

One of my favorite pastoral retorts on this topic was from Pastor Mark Crow, a good friend of mine from Oklahoma City. A person in his church approached him and said, "I wasn't getting much out of the worship," and he said, "I'm sorry. We weren't worshipping you."

A key part of gaining relevance is speaking the audience's language. As more Christians begin to realize that the power of the Holy Spirit gives us the ability to relate to our culture, and it's acceptable to be culturally relevant without compromising our beliefs, I believe we will see even greater salvations and other miracles throughout our churches.

THE GIFTS OF THE SPIRIT IN CHURCH LIFE

When I arrived at my church in Virginia Beach in 1999, some in the church were behaving in the manner I just warned against. They were seeking signs, and they were stuck in the past, behaving in a routine fashion, conditioned to respond to "Holy Spirit" moments in the service. One of the first things I noticed in the auditorium was two long strips of brown tape across the front of the stage area, stuck to the carpet. It resembled packing tape, and the two strips were about six or seven feet apart. This puzzled me. The tape was dirty; it was twisted and wrinkled in spots. It simply didn't look good. Plus, my desire is to have a beautiful church that honors God and is inviting to guests. In my opinion, a couple long strips of dirty packing tape across the front of the church wasn't beautiful, didn't honor God, and would probably be distracting, if not disgusting, to visitors.

When the tape was removed, many people became absolutely distressed. They were moaning about the disappearance of the "renewal tape." I asked them to repeat the words. "Renewal tape." I had no clue what renewal tape was, so I asked Pastor Robert Cameron, a great friend of mine, and a pastor on our staff. He's also a fantastic singer with multiple albums recorded. I pulled Robert aside and asked him about the renewal tape. I was new to the church and wanted to know how to respond, though regardless of what he said, the tape wasn't coming back!

He explained to me that the renewal tape was placed on the ground so that people knew where to line up for prayer. The distance between the two strips of tape was to allow room for people to fall down when the Holy Spirit touched them. This had obviously become conditioned behavior for some of the people. At some point, the Holy Spirit had blessed them, and they tried to remain in that moment. As this chapter explains, God moves. God had certainly moved on and had no interest in the church having dirty, wrinkly tape all over the front of the auditorium.

After hearing the reason for the tape, and recognizing the lack of understanding among some of the people for the entire purpose of the church—to reach the lost—I got up on Sunday and explained the need to move on. The great part about God is he works well in all things, for those who love Him and are called according to His purposes.[54] I was able to repeatedly use the example of the tape on the floor to motivate our church to keep looking for ways to draw the lost.

I remember saying over and over, "Get off the floor. Go out into the streets and let's reach the people who need Jesus."

The gifts of the Holy Spirit are significant and vital. They are meant to be utilized to encourage Christians and to reach the lost. Pastors and leaders must order their services with an eye to remaining relevant and understood by the culture. We must not offend unbelievers while remaining strong in the truth of our convictions and the message of the gospel of Jesus. When we stop chasing signs and wonders and preach His Word, miracles will happen—and the greatest miracle of all is the salvation of a lost soul.

DEVELOP THE GIFTS OF THE SPIRIT

1. If God stopped speaking to you, how long would it take to notice?
2. Is there a consistent pattern of miracles, signs and wonders following what you believe?
3. When you speak to those who do not know Jesus, are you asking the Holy Spirit to help make you relevant to help your witness?
4. Are you familiar with the person of the Holy Spirit and how He works in your life, the church and the world?

YOUR DESTINY IS CONNECTED TO YOUR LEADER

Have confidence in your leaders and submit to their authority, because they keep watch over you as those who must give an account. Do this so that their work will be a joy, not a burden, for that would be of no benefit to you.

Hebrews 13:17

In life, it's not always what you do that counts, but who you do it with. God has ordained relationships for every person to fulfill his or her destiny by staying connected to the right leader. Often, it is the words of the leader alone that will sustain you. Yet people often abandon a God-ordained relationship prematurely because they get offended by leadership style. Burden does not necessitate timing. The manner of your last exit determines your next entrance. Honor leadership and see your destiny fulfilled.

I don't know what your destiny will be, but one thing I know: the only ones among you who will be truly fulfilled are those who will have sought and found how to serve.

—Albert Schweitzer

YOUR DESTINY IS ALL ABOUT
YOUR GOD-ORDAINED ATTACHMENTS

Throughout nature, we can see many examples of living creatures and plants that have a relationship with the sky, the water, or the earth. That relationship is their God-designed atmosphere. It is the environment that God has ordained for them to be attached. This God-ordained attachment provides life, protection, and opportunities for growth. A simple example is a flower. Flowers are beautiful. We give them as gifts or in memorial of a loved one. So long as the flower remains in its Godordained attachment, the soil, it flourishes. Some flowers can bloom and remain for months at a time. Some bloom for just one day. But, regardless of its life span, as soon as a flower is removed from its God-ordained attachment, it begins to die. No matter how long we keep it in water, refrigerated, and even sprinkle in some vitamin powder, that flower will die sooner than it would have if it had remained in its God-ordained attachment.

People are like flowers. As long as they remain in their God-ordained attachment, they can receive life, protection, and opportunities for growth. Psalm 92:13 tells us, "They that are planted in the house of the Lord shall flourish…"

Pastor Paul Scanlon, who pastors a great church in England, often speaks about the significance of a Christian remaining in his or her Godordained attachment, which is the local church God has called him or her to join.

I've heard Pastor Scanlon say, "A sick fish is still better off in water than out of water." What a great analogy for Christian life. As long as that fish remains in the water, no matter how sick it is, it still has a better chance of surviving than if it were removed from the water. The water is its natural environment. It's the God-designed atmosphere wherein the fish is intended to live and function and fulfill the activity for which it's designed.

Unfortunately, the church often takes its sick fish, the Christians who have made mistakes or have fallen into sin, and tosses them out of the water. Time after time, I have seen hurting, dying Christians limp into our church because they were kicked out of the one God-designed atmosphere in which they could receive life and healing—the church! I don't believe this element of faith is nearly as high a priority among Christians as it should be.

I have also seen Christians become offended in church life and remove themselves from the God-ordained environment. They limp away, without attempting to resolve the issue, and they wander around, wounded and hurting. All the while healing could be found in the local church where they were planted by God.

The vital importance of remaining connected to the local church—especially when we are wounded—is hard to overstate.

Of course, if the church itself is the cause of the hurt, and its pastors or leaders committed a legitimate wrong, then if reconciliation is not possible, a person should move on. But even if that were the case, I believe with all my heart that we need to make sure that we understand that our destiny is connected to our leader, and we ought not to touch anointed leadership God has appointed. A great example of the necessity of allowing God to correct His appointed leaders is explicitly demonstrated by the example of David and King Saul. 1 Samuel 24:1-7 says:

> Now it happened, when Saul had returned from following the Philistines, that it was told him, saying, "Take note! David is in the Wilderness of En Gedi." Then Saul took three thousand chosen men from all Israel, and went to seek David and his men on the Rocks of the Wild Goats. So he came to the sheepfolds by the road, where there was a cave; and Saul went in to attend to his needs. (David and his men were staying in the recesses of the cave.) Then the men of David said to him, "This is the day of which the LORD said to you, 'Behold, I will deliver your enemy into your hand, that you may do to him as it seems good to you.'" And David arose and secretly cut off a corner of Saul's robe. Now it happened afterward that David's heart troubled him because he had cut Saul's robe. And he said to his men, "The LORD forbid that I should do this thing to my master, the LORD's anointed, to stretch out my hand against him, seeing he is the anointed of the LORD." So David restrained his servants with these words, and did not allow them to rise against Saul. And Saul got up from the cave and went on his way.

Saul and an army of three thousand men chased David into the wilderness. Saul had already attempted to kill him by throwing a javelin at him. David had already been anointed to be the next king. The people of Israel favored him over Saul. They sang about David's great conquests in battle. David had every reason to defend himself and had no reason to fear repercussions if he were to kill Saul.

Now David found himself hiding in a cave, and King Saul enters that very same cave to relieve himself. David's men were ecstatic, because this was the opportunity to kill their pursuer. At first, David listened to his men. He crept up unnoticed by Saul. David cut a piece of Saul's overcoat off. Immediately, his heart was convicted, for he had raised his hand against God's anointed king. David was called to serve under Saul. His destiny was connected to that man, and David realized that it was God's choice as to the timing of David receiving the kingdom.

Until God releases you from the leadership He's chosen for you, you run the risk of limiting your potential by abandoning your post early. We should learn from David. Even when he had the opportunity to attack Saul, he realized that it was up to God when Saul would be removed. It's not your decision as to the timing of removing a disobedient leader. Sometimes people can become offended and walk away from the Godordained attachment in pursuit of their own destiny, but little do they know they're sabotaging their own destiny by not remaining in that Godordained attachment, or at least not trying to resolve what needs to be resolved in a submissive, loyal way with a dedicated heart toward that leader so they can move on into their destiny.

Pastors are not immune to the challenge of overcoming offenses and remaining connected to God-ordained attachments. Senior pastors also must remain committed to remaining connected to their leaders. Whether it's denominational oversight, a network of churches, or perhaps it's key relationships with other leaders who have influence in and over our lives, we can all fall prey to the challenge of remaining submitted. Finally, within the local church, associate pastors and leaders must work at remaining submitted and serving in their Godordained attachments. Refusing and purposing in your heart to not become offended at leadership style is a very important commitment all leaders must make. Always remember the great honor it is to lead God's church, and remember God has ordained the connection to your leader. Trust Him in the good times and the challenging moments.

THE FULFILLMENT OF DESTINY
DEMANDS OVERCOMING OFFENSES

The connection to your God-ordained leader is important, and rare is the career in which that connection isn't challenged at some point. Even John the Baptist, whom Jesus said was the greatest man ever born, had an occasion recorded in the Bible when he struggled to remain submissive to the vision of his leader—and his leader was Jesus! [55] The moment occurred while John was in prison. He was alone. He was vulnerable. He sent his friends and disciples to ask Jesus if He was the Messiah.[56] John is about to face certain death, and he realizes his job, his very purpose on earth was to make people ready for the Messiah.

He heard about the people Jesus was ministering to, and he questioned whether Jesus really was the Messiah! This is the same John who had baptized Jesus, seen the dove of the Holy Spirit descend, and heard the voice of God say, "This is my beloved Son."[57]

How did John go from announcing Jesus was the Messiah and hearing God announce that Jesus was His Son, to questioning Jesus' deity? [58] Let's go back to the beginning.

John's birth announcement was supernatural. Like Isaac, Samson, and Jesus, John's parents received a pre-natal visit from an angel. In Luke 1 we find the record of this event. Zacharias and Elizabeth were barren and had lost hope for children. Gabriel appeared and told Zacharias that Elizabeth would have a son who would be the forerunner of the Messiah. He would come in the spirit and the power of Elijah. We know that John's father was unable to speak until the day that John was born because he didn't believe the words of the angel Gabriel. Zacharias was mute for six months, but when he finally was able to speak, he made sure that they named their son John, for that was what Gabriel had instructed to be the baby's name.

We also know that John had lived a life of separation from the world. He was there to make the path straight and to get people ready for the coming of the Messiah. He had a very unusual diet. He lived out in the wilderness. He was a voice crying in the wilderness. He fulfilled the prophecy of Isaiah, who wrote "The voice of one crying in the wilderness: prepare the way of the Lord; make His paths straight."[59] John made disciples, and he baptized people into the baptism of repentance. He lived a live of separation and a life of holiness. He was bold, he was direct, and he was confrontational. He was a strong, prophetic voice who was passionately committed to getting people ready for the Messiah.

At some point in his ministry, the people sent the priests to find out if John was the Messiah or by what power he spoke. John sensed they were getting overly enamored with him, and he said, "I'm not the Messiah. I'm just here to make you ready for the Messiah. When he comes, I will not be worthy to loosen His sandals. Don't think I'm the man. I'm just here to get you ready for the man. The Lamb of God? He's the man. You think I'm something incredible? Wait until He comes. He's the Messiah. I'm just trying to get you ready for the Messiah."[60]

We have no doubt John understood that his role was to serve to make the way ready for Jesus.

To recap: John had an angel announce his birth and purpose. John embraced his purpose and lived a life of separation and piety. John preached with fire and conviction that Jesus was the Messiah. John witnessed the Holy Spirit as a dove and heard the voice of the Father declaring Jesus was the Son of God. He declared plainly and repeatedly that Jesus was the One whom the Jews had been looking for from the beginning of time. Oh, and by the way, Jesus was his cousin.[61]

After all those experiences and after a life of ministering, John found himself in prison, near the end of his life. He was having second thoughts. The only passage we have to determine the source of John's doubt is recorded in Matthew 11:2-3. It says, "And when John heard in prison about *the works of Christ*, he sent two of his disciples and said to Him, 'Are You the Coming One or do we look for another'?" (emphasis added). Perhaps John heard not only about Christ's work, but he heard about the types of people Jesus allowed to be around him. Over and over again, the Pharisees remarked about Jesus hanging out with sinners.

John took a vow never to drink alcohol. He hears Jesus is turning water into wine. John lived a life according to the traditions of the Jewish covenant, and he lived it as close to perfect as he could. Jesus has got a reputation of being a friend of sinners, and His disciples don't seem to observe the traditions of the Pharisees. John is hearing that Jesus is spending time with sinners and prostitutes, and he's heard that Jesus is doing things in a very unconventional way. It's very likely that John is offended by Jesus' leadership style. It's very likely that John pictured the Messiah doing ministeryin a fashion similar to John's. He probably thought, *This is not what I pictured the Messiah to be. This is not what I pictured leadership to look like. This is not at all anything like I imagined.*

Very often, as we grow in leadership, we will face a situation or an opportunity where the senior pastor or the leadership will do something unconventional or enter into a ministry avenue that is either not how we would do it or is controversial. The test of our commitment to fulfilling our destiny lies in our ability to remain submitted, to overcome the opportunity to take offense. So long as the leaders are not operating immorally, illegally, or un-scripturally, we should not abandon our God-ordained leadership over an issue of style. The true test of our heart happens in these moments, and the fulfillment of our destiny is furthered by the right response.

Of course, when John sends his disciples to question Jesus, the Lord gives a brilliant answer. And it's in Christ's answer that we find the measure to use when evaluating our own ability to avoid taking offense when our leaders do something unconventional.

He says to John's disciples, "Go and tell John the things which you hear and see: The blind see and the lame walk; the lepers are cleansed and the deaf hear; the dead are raised up and the poor have the gospel preached to them. And blessed is he who is not offended because of Me."[62] Jesus pointed out the results of His ministry, not the techniques employed. In effect, He was saying, "You can tell John what's really happening. You may not like the way I do it, but the gospel is being preached. People are being healed. The results speak for themselves. It may not be the way you do it, John, but it's the work of God nonetheless." And he concludes His message to John with the most powerful point—blessed is he who is not offended because of Me.

Jesus tells us that there is a blessing by not getting offended by the style of your leadership. Quite often we face the temptation of thinking, *If I were the boss, I wouldn't do that.* But the point is you're not the boss, and your destiny is connected to that leader. And if you want to have a confidence in your future and a guarantee of your success, always understand the importance of honoring your leadership. Understand the Godgiven attachments that God has put in and over your life. I believe submission is not proven in agreement. If we agree on a matter, neither of us is submitting to the other. Submission means to get under the mission. And I believe submission is only ever proven in disagreement.

Passing the test of this principle is vital to the fulfillment of your destiny. Can you overcome offenses? Can you still submit to your leaders when you don't agree with their methodology? I don't believe if any leader is asking you to do something that's illegal you should do it. I don't believe if any leader is asking you to do something that's immoral you should do it. I certainly believe if a leader is asking you to do something that is outside of the theological wisdom of Scripture, you should not do it. I believe those are the boundaries that we ought not to cross.

If, however, your leaders are preaching the gospel and souls are being saved, albeit through methods you would not have chosen, you face the same test that John the Baptist faced. Listen to the words of Jesus in these situations and choose to submit to your leadership. What you sow in those moments, you will reap in your own leadership. If you can remember, as Jesus reminded John, that it's the results that matter more than style, you will see your destiny fulfilled.

YOUR LAST EXIT IS YOUR NEXT ENTRANCE

Unfortunately, I've seen many leaders get offended by a senior pastor, and as a result of that offense, prematurely answered what eventually might have been a call of God to be the senior pastor or founding pastor of a church. I've often heard it said that the way you leave your last season determines the way in which you start your next season. I wholeheartedly believe if you don't leave your last position well, you can't have great confidence that God will bless your next venture. I have seen so many people answer a call prematurely, move on early, and sabotage their own destiny. If they only understood how critically connected their destiny is to that leader. God will not open the door they are trying to enter if they slammed the one they just left in the senior pastor's face!

I have also seen people leave poorly, yet from the outside it looks like they are prospering. This can be difficult to reconcile, but God is the ultimate judge. He sees into a man or woman's heart. In the end, there is a big difference between character and talent, and time reveals all.

David said, "I'd rather be a doorkeeper in the house of the Lord than dwell in the tents of the wicked. One day in the house of God is better than a thousand elsewhere."[63] It's better to be a greeter in the parking lot of the church, exposed to the elements, than to be in the VIP lounge at the finest party club in the city. Often, a person who abandons the church where God has planted him leaves because he desires a bigger platform or a certain title. I'd rather be a part of a house that's flourishing and thriving and not consumed with opportunity and title and position. When it's time to move on, if it ever is, allow God to make that move and honor your leadership as you leave. How we make these life transitions is as important as the transition itself.

In my own life, I believe I honored the senior pastor at my first assignment in ministry. I served as a senior associate pastor at a great church for ten years. I didn't necessarily want to leave, but I had to in order for God to fulfill my destiny. After exiting properly, I was approached by Hills Christian Life Center, now known as Hillsong Church, to become the Bible college director. During my interview with the associate pastor, Mike Murphy, I said, "I'll come for two years, and then I feel God has called me to America."

But soon, I realized my time for America had not yet arrived. Sure enough, eight years later, I was still part of Hills Christian Life Center. I remember the day that I felt like it was time for me to go to America. Even though Sharon and I both felt like God had opened the door and we felt it was right, we still submitted that to our senior pastors Brian and Bobbie Houston and asked them if they felt this was the will of God. We knew our destiny was connected to our leaders. We spoke with Brian and Bobbie and said, "Look, we're stirred for this, but if for any reason you don't feel like this is right, we won't go." They agreed with our feeling and blessed us as we properly exited Australia to enter America.

There's a huge difference between people who went away on their own and those who were sent with the blessing of their leaders. Don't preempt the work of God in your life by allowing personal agenda or ambition to drive you away without your leadership's blessing. Some of us are truly called to remain a team member for our whole ministry life or volunteer leadership life. Some of us are called to go on and build a new church, or build another church. Wait for that calling. Remember your last exit is your next entrance. If you are willing to wait for the proper timing, and you exit with the blessing of your senior pastors, your next position of leadership will be greatly blessed.

BURDEN DOES NOT NECESSITATE TIMING

If you leave, the manner of your exit is very important in establishing your new start. Just as important is the timing of your departure. We've all heard it said hundreds of times: "Timing is everything." The Bible is full of stories of men and women who were anxious to accomplish what God had called them to do (sometimes with an audible voice), yet had to wait much longer than they expected to see it come to pass. Just because God declared an opportunity, it doesn't mean He's ready for us to do it today. I think we can all relate to the story of Moses, who learned quite well that burden does not necessitate timing.

Moses was set up to be the rescuer of Israel practically from birth. Think about the circumstances of his early years. Pharaoh had ordered that all Israelite newborn boys be killed. Moses was saved from destruction, and not only that, Pharaoh's own daughter adopted him![64] Moses was raised in Pharaoh's house and was given access to the knowledge, training, and culture of Egypt. Later in life, when God asked him to approach Pharaoh, Moses had easy access and knowledge of the customs of the court by virtue of his upbringing. His early rescue and training prepared him for a mission that would not take place for over forty-to-fifty years.

Of course, Moses was human, just like you and me. He wanted to rescue his brothers, the Israelites, from the oppression of the Egyptians. He saw how unique his position was in the land, and he had a burden for the children of Israel. He was ready to rescue them, even if it was only one at a time. He was tired of watching the Israelites being persecuted and demeaned. After a short while, one day he could bear no longer to witness the mistreatment of the Israelites. He was called to help them, and he was going to help! So the next time he saw an Egyptian beating a Jew, he waited for the right moment, and he killed the Egyptian and buried him in the sand![65]

How often do we feel compassion for a need or a call to a cause and jump blindly in, fists swinging? We want to impetuously rush out and "do something" rather than develop strategy and wisdom or get proper training. We see in the story of Moses how this type of rash behavior will most likely backfire. He thought he was helping the Israelites, but instead, he left them with a negative impression of a violent, hostile man.

Shortly after he murdered the Egyptian, two Hebrew men were arguing. Moses approached them to break up the fight, and they asked him, "Are you going to kill us like you killed the Egyptian?"[66] Moses was so disillusioned with the response and the lack of appreciation, as well as the fear of Pharaoh finding out, that he had to leave Egypt and the Israelites. He had prematurely tried to answer the call of God, and by taking matters into his own hands, he had blown his chance at rescuing the Israelites anytime soon.

Now, instead of leading a rebellion against the Egyptians, as he believed he was going to do, Moses was tending sheep in the desert. Finally, after forty years in the desert with a bunch of animals, God spoke to Moses. Forty years! Alone, with sheep! Finally, God appears in a burning bush and says, "Now it's time for you to go back to Egypt and tell Pharaoh, 'Let my people go.'"[67]

Four decades earlier, Moses had a burden for Israel and a desire to stop the oppression of his people. He had acted on that desire by killing a single Egyptian for hurting a Jew. He didn't realize that God's desire wasn't for Moses to help the Israelites one person at a time. God wanted to bring the whole nation of Israel out of Egypt. Moses's burden in and of itself did not necessitate timing.

As you read this, you can probably relate to Moses's experience. You can be the right person with the right burden but have the wrong timing. In those moments, we can look back at examples like Moses, Joseph, Daniel, and others and realize that no matter how stirred we are for God's call, until He pushes the "go" button, we will be ineffective and end up frustrated. Your destiny is connected to your leaders, and learning to listen to their counsel as far as timing of a move or ministry opportunity will serve you well. Burden does not, in and of itself, ever necessitate timing.

HONOR YOUR LEADER AND YOUR DESTINY IS FULFILLED

In Chapter 2, the story of Miriam and Aaron's rebellion against Moses served as an illustration of honor. It's such a powerful illustration of the connection to a leader that I had to include it here as well. God placed Moses in the position of the senior leader, and God placed Miriam and Aaron to serve as second in command. Moses was their leader, but they were seeking to be Moses's equal.

It's interesting how the God-ordained ultimate authority of Moses is revealed by Aaron's response to Miriam's affliction with leprosy. Shortly after the Lord came down and told Miriam and Aaron how wrong they were for challenging Moses about his Cushite wife, then afflicted Miriam with leprosy, we read of Aaron's desperate plea to Moses. "Oh, my lord! Please do not lay this sin on us, in which we have done foolishly and in which we have sinned. Please do not let her be as one dead, whose flesh is half consumed when he comes out of his mother's womb!"[68]

In this petition to Moses, Aaron is reestablishing the position and recognizing the position of Moses's leadership in and over his life. He's calling him "my lord." He begs Moses to forgive them. Aaron admits his foolishness. He realized as a result of God's swift, angry response that his choice to speak against Moses actually was sinful, and he is repenting. Aaron and Miriam brought a complaint about Moses's wife, but in reality they were attempting to supplant him. They did not honor their leader. This action of rebellion certainly limited their ability to see their own destinies fulfilled. In fact, if it weren't for the mercy of Moses, God likely would have killed them.

Just as Miriam and Aaron used the pretext of Moses's wife in their challenge of his leadership, often people will bring a surface complaint against their spiritual leader in an attempt to avoid addressing the real issue. One thing I know after nearly thirty years in ministry: the initial claimed problem is never really the problem. There's always a deeper problem. If you dig below the surface, there's usually a lot more to it—personal agendas, selfish ambition, seeking an equal position of leadership. Usually, it's a sinful, prideful attitude. Moses cries out to God, "Please heal her," and God healed her but said in the process, "if I was her father, I would have spat in her face."[69] God despised the actions of Miriam and Aaron because they were really committing the sin of pride—the downfall of Lucifer—under the pretext of complaining about Moses's choice for a wife.

Honoring your leader is a critical part of developing your destiny. In the New Testament, the story of Paul and Barnabas demonstrates how a destiny can be cut short when a person fails to honor his leader.

In Acts 13:1-3, the Holy Spirit said, "Separate unto me Paul and Barnabus for the work which I have called them." They fasted and prayed and were sent off into their missionary journeys. Paul was in the process of becoming the most powerful leader of that era and ended up writing twothirds of the New Testament. Barnabas was called by God to be his right-hand man. In fact, when Paul frightened all the other disciples, as they knew he had persecuted Christians, it was Barnabas who vouched for Paul's conversion. Barnabas served to be the bridge for Paul to cross over from persecutor to persecuted.[70] Barnabas told the other disciples about the sermons he had heard Paul preach and explained to the disciples that Paul was trustworthy.

Paul and Barnabas experienced powerful, effective ministry together. But, for some reason, we read of a sharp disagreement just two chapters after the Holy Spirit called them.[71] Paul was the set man, the senior pastor, if you will. Barnabas was very important in serving God by serving Paul. As they prepared to go on a long missions trip, Barnabus suggested that they bring John Mark, a man who had ministered with them in the past.

Paul did not want to take John Mark with them, but Barnabus did. They had such a sharp disagreement that they parted company. Barnabas left his leader. He did not honor Paul by submitting to Paul's decision. Barnabas had opened the door for Paul to enter the ministry, the Holy Spirit had appointed them to work together, and I believe that Barnabus walked out of a Godordained relationship. He's never heard from again. And the writer of Acts does not follow the works of Barnabus but follows the works of the Apostle Paul and records out the rest of the missionary journeys of the Apostle Paul and Paul's imprisonment. And then Paul writes all the Paulian epistles to individuals and churches. Barnabas left and was never heard from again.

Though it isn't always easy to honor a leader, especially when you disagree, it is essential to your destiny. Think about the God-ordained attachments in your life. Be thankful and honoring, because your destiny is connected to that leader. So as we think about this, think: *Stay planted in the relationships that God has called you to be a part of, and watch your destiny be fulfilled.*

YOUR DESTINY, YOUR LEADER IN CHURCH LIFE

During my early years as a Christian, I was naïve in a lot of areas of church leadership and culture. I came into a church that had been built by a pastor who was a renowned man of God. Television programs like *60 Minutes* would frequently come to services to record amazing miracles that were happening under his ministry. I entered this church as its leadership was being transitioned to a new senior pastor. The new pastor was a phenomenal preacher. He was a great storyteller. He was such a powerful storyteller that people would often stand up in church in a physical response to his words. I remember a time when he was relating a story about a blind man about to walk off a cliff, and people shouted out, "Stop!" as though the man was really there, about to fall.

He was a gifted orator and a great pastor, and I loved him with all my heart. I was soon asked to become the youth pastor. God was gracious, and we began to grow. It wasn't long until we had over three hundred teenagers in our Saturday night meetings. I was completely consumed with building the youth ministry. We were growing, and the church was in a building project. It was organized chaos as we tried to contain the growth and manage the influx of people.

I remember occasionally hearing complaints that our church wasn't healthy. My initial response was to tell people to honor our pastor, to follow the vision, and to build the church. In hindsight, I realize the church got so busy with a building project that the people began neglecting their other responsibilities. Our lives had lost balance. We were literally building the new church by ourselves. We didn't hire an outside construction company. We laid the bricks, and we poured the concrete! I even used my own car to tow the asphalt, which left it covered with black spray. Our church lost its focus on people and was solely focused on the building.

It couldn't last. Eventually, I found myself in a meeting with other leaders who were chastising our pastor. I was shocked to hear some of the attitudes and mean-spirited comments that people made in confrontation of the senior pastor's vision. I watched our senior pastor remain humble and publicly apologize to the church for allowing us to lose our focus on reaching people. I learned something that day about humility in the heart of a senior pastor. I also learned that no matter what he did, some people were never going to be pleased.

Things were never the same after that confrontation. In spite of the senior pastor's apology and efforts to change, he continued to repeat some of the same mistakes. The pressures of his choices and management style began to take its toll on his physical body. After awhile, he began taking extended breaks, leaving me in charge of the church for up to two months at a time.

My goal was always to have the church be healthy and growing when he returned. I had no aspirations to be the senior pastor. I wanted to serve him—I wanted to be like Jonathan was for David.

Eventually, as he continued to deteriorate, I realized that I needed to move on before I started to become disloyal to him. I didn't want to lose my respect for him, but he was becoming less emotionally healthy with each passing month. He began to focus on negative external problems, and my heart was excited for growth and opportunities. I knew I had to resign so that I could be loyal to him.

And so, I resigned. I had turned in my resignation and said good-bye when I was approached by one of the church elders. He came to my house late that same night and said, "If you stay, if you'll withdraw your resignation, we'll remove the senior pastor and appoint you to be pastor."

I was so offended by his disloyalty to his pastor that I didn't even let him in the front door of my house. I replied, "Not only will I not accept your invitation—because God appointed this man, and I have no intention to replace him—but I will also inform the senior pastor of what I believe to be a seditious spirit. I am going to tell him that you had this conversation with me."

Some people might think I overreacted. Some people probably would have taken the offer. I could not. I would not. I know without a doubt that my destiny was connected to my leader, and had I chosen to join in the plot to cast him aside, I would never have seen my destiny fulfilled with God's blessing.

DEVELOP YOUR DESTINY, STAY CONNECTED

1. Are you more concerned with *what* you are doing than *whom* you are working with? Do you believe that God works through the relationships in your life more than He works through a job or project?
2. Do you trust the words of your leader? What about when you disagree? Are you able to submit (except if asked to be immoral, illegal, or un-scriptural) when you disagree?
3. Have you ever been like Miriam and Aaron? Has anyone every done something similar to you? Don't allow yourself to desire a position for which God hasn't called you.

4. Do you currently feel burdened but aren't yet released to serve in that area? Are you willing to grow and wait for the timing of God? Are you able to finish what you're currently working on until God says it's time to answer His call?

HAVE YOU COME TO HELP?

So we built the wall…for the people had a heart and mind to work [help].

Nehemiah 4:6

In many organizations, especially the church, leaders fail to teach people how to enter a position of leadership. Too often the newest to arrive are given a sense of prominence if they have an ability to fill a perceived need. The best leaders are often trained in the organization and arise from within, although God also brings mature leaders in from other places, because He has great blessing to pour out and needs more leaders to get the job done. Whether from within or without, we must train our leaders to approach every opportunity from a selfless perspective that says, "I'm here to help!"

Coming together is a beginning. Keeping together is progress. Working together is success.

—Henry Ford

David went out to meet them, and said to them, "If you come peacefully *to help me*, my heart shall be united with you…

1 Chronicles 12:17a (emphasis added)

NOBODY IS INDISPENSABLE

A critical lesson that our churches need to internalize is that *nobody is indispensable*. It's important to value people and appreciate their service, but we must avoid allowing anyone (including the leadership) to believe that a specific individual is responsible for growth. Jesus says, "I will build my church…"[72] He did not say that Pastor Jones or Leader Smith would build the church. It's His church and He will build it. And He will only use people who remain humble.

Sometimes people in the church get excited about the talents of a new leader and can (intentionally or not) give the new leader the impression that she is "saving" the church. We cannot allow people to enter leadership with the notion that they are rescuing the church and without them the church would be in trouble and would not be able to grow. If we aren't careful, we can allow people to feel like they are bringing the anointing, and until they arrived, there was no anointing. We must teach them that they are blessed to serve, they are appreciated, but no one is indispensable.

David shows how to handle this situation in 1 Chronicles 12:818. This story tells us that David was holed up in the desert. He was hiding from Saul, who had repeatedly attempted to kill him. David was certainly not in a position of strength. He was tired, prone to fear, and running for his life. Suddenly, some incredible soldiers show up to join his team. They are described as "brave warriors, ready for battle and able to handle the shield and spear. Their faces were the faces of lions, and they were as swift as gazelles."[73] The Bible adds that these were commanders. The lowest ranked commander was in charge of a hundred soldiers and some commanded a battalion of a thousand. To put this in a modern context, these guys were like Navy SEALS. They were Army Rangers or Delta Force. David went out to meet them. He didn't shout with excitement and thank them profusely. He didn't tell them he didn't know what would have happened if they hadn't arrived. He says, "Have you come to help me?" Then he says, just so they know he is not pleading for their aid, that if they came to betray him, then may God "bring judgment."[74]

These were highly skilled men. In a church setting, these are the type of people who built great buildings or were worldrenowned singers or worship leaders, business leaders, or children's ministry leaders who had experienced great success. In spite of his dire circumstances and despite the great qualifications of these men, David didn't say, "Boy, have we been praying for you. We have been desperate for you." But isn't that what we do in church? We find out someone is a great sound technician, for example, and we exclaim, "Oh, we're so glad to have you."

We have to teach them to have a heart that asks, "How can I help?" We must teach them first how to come into church and how to join a team. Then we can train them in how to join a staff or how to become a leader who surrenders his personal agenda and his own ambition and serves the vision of the house. They must be trained to begin each day with the question, "How can I help?"

PEOPLE MUST BE TRAINED FOR LEADERSHIP

Now that I've established the priority of understanding leadership culture and the importance of realizing that your destiny is connected to your leader, I want to focus on how to enter a leadership position. I believe there is an absence of teaching resources available to show a person how he should prepare himself for becoming a staff member at a church or a volunteer leader in any organization. In the workplace and in our schools, we have orientation weekends or extensive training systems. In the most important organization on earth, the church of Jesus Christ, we just toss people into a position and expect them to thrive. They may have the natural aptitude or the spiritual discernment to survive and even flourish in their position, but without training on how to interact with leadership, they will never realize their full potential.

First, we need to have an attitude that radiates a desire to serve the vision of the leaders. Our primary aim is to take the vision of the senior leadership and bring it to life in our sphere of influence. We are not there to build our personal ministry. We are there to build the church and to follow the direction of the God-appointed senior pastors.

Sometimes we can learn from other people's mistakes. The following illustration demonstrates how *not* to enter leadership.

Prior to becoming a senior pastor in America, I served on a team in a church in Australia. I was near the front of the church after a service, and a man approached me. He was a musician, and he came from another state and moved up to be part of our church. He said to me, "I want you to know I really like you. I have no problems with you. I have no issues with you." I thought this was an unusual conversation for the circumstances, and I think he revealed more about himself by what he didn't say. The way he was expressing himself led me to believe that while he was saying he liked me, he was setting up the conversation, as he was about to begin talking about someone that he didn't like.

Sure enough, after he had attempted to flatter me, he started talking about the music in the church and how as a musician he really felt like his involvement in the worship team could really bring a new style to our worship. He wanted me to know that he could take our worship to a higher level. In essence, he was saying that our current worship team and worship pastor weren't as good as he was.

I interrupted him mid-conversation and said, "Listen, there are thousands of people in this church who love this church, and the church is growing really, really well. And if you've come to this church just to change it into what you want it to be, then you need to go back to the church you came from. If that's how worship was in your former church, what are you doing here? Don't try to come here to change this church into something you think it should be. If you want to really be a part of this church, you should be here saying, 'I'm here to serve the vision. How can I help?'"

He quickly realized that I wasn't going to tolerate any undermining of the senior leaders that I was there to serve. In no uncertain terms, I gave him a tutorial in how to enter into leadership. Unfortunately, he didn't (like most of us) get the point after the first lesson. He then started speaking badly about the senior pastor who had brought me on as a staff pastor years before. I was committed to serving my senior pastor. He felt like he was just explaining some areas that were wrong with the church. But he kept adding, "I have no problem with you."

I finally stopped him for good and said, "Listen, you may have no problem with me, but I have a huge problem with you. And if you think you can sit here and speak badly about the senior pastor who I'm serving in this church, then you need to re-evaluate the situation. If you think you can approach me, and by including the point that you like me believe that I will automatically put you in positions of leadership and change our worship and change the music, you are definitely wrong." I concluded our conversation with the recommendation that he return to his previous church, as it was obvious that our church had far too many problems. He tried to enter leadership by pointing out what he perceived to be problems that he could either personally improve or help give us tips for improvement. His approach was the complete opposite of the proper approach in entering leadership.

When entering leadership, a person needs to abandon personal agendas or individual desires. They need to surrender their ambitions to the directives of the church leadership. By serving the vision of the church leadership, over time they will cultivate the gifts God placed in them and will ultimately become all that God designed. Enter leadership with a spirit of humility and service, and begin each day by asking, "How can I help?"

This same attitude will serve you well in the workplace. Whether your employer or supervisor is a Christian, your loyalty and effort to build their vision should be complete. If God has placed you in a relationship (even in a marriage) with a non-believer, the Bible tells us to pray for them, and over time your love for God could be the very attribute that draws them into a relationship with Jesus Christ.

GOD ESTABLISHES LEADERS FROM WITHIN AND WITHOUT

I've heard many pastors teach that we must work with what's "in our hands." This point is made to help us look within the house of God for leaders. I believe the best people you can raise up in your church are the people that are sons and daughters of your church. By sons and daughters, I mean people who have been in your church for an established period of time and who have been trained with the principles contained in this book. It is a wonderful thing to see a young person raised in the church, who has the true heart of the church, be given the opportunity to lead.

Sometimes new people, especially mature Christians, come from other churches with their preconceptions about how church should be led. They struggle to make adjustments and fully adopt and endorse the leadership of the church, and they end up creating disunity among the leadership team. When we quickly give newly arrived but mature Christians leadership positions, we end up empowering people that might not yet have the heart of the church. They're not sons of the house. They can be adopted into the church, but like a natural adoption, that process takes time.

I don't mean to imply that God will not send leaders from outside your church from time to time. He does, and He will. A great example of this is found in 2 Kings 4:1-7. This passage tells the story of a widow woman who came to Elisha with a desperate plea—she had lost her husband and was about to lose her two sons as slaves to pay the creditors. And Elisha said, "How can I help?" Even Elisha, the great prophet, had the right attitude. He asked her how he could serve. Elisha asked her what she had left. She responded, "Absolutely nothing but a little jar of oil."

Elisha instructed her to go around the neighborhood and ask everyone for empty jars. He told her, "Do not gather just a few." She went around, gathering all the jars she could. She brought them home and followed Elisha's instruction to pour the oil that she had into the jars. God worked a miracle, as the oil kept flowing into every jar she had brought into the house. When all the jars were full, she told her son to bring her another jar. He replied, "There are no jars left." At his word, the oil stopped flowing. She told Elisha what happened, and he told her to sell the oil to pay the creditors. She and her sons were saved and were able to withstand a famine because God brought vessels from outside her house.

This miraculous story teaches us two leadership truths:

1. You can bring people from the outside, and God will cause people to come from the outside because of the magnitude of the anointing that's about to be released.
2. When they come, teach them that they didn't bring the anointing. They were brought by God to help handle the anointing.

The oil is representative of God's anointing. God had so much blessing and overflow of anointing that He was prepared to pour out for this woman that He told her to go get more vessels. She didn't have enough containers within her house to capture the abundant goodness and provision that He was about to release in the life of her house. When an overflowing anointing of God is about to be released in your local church, the Lord can arrange for extra vessels to come in from outside.

Notice that the direct source of the blessing was already in her house. She had the oil. She didn't have much, but she had enough for God to use. The source of the oil (anointing) that flowed into all the extra vessels that she gathered was a little vessel that had been in her house all along. God delights in pouring out his anointing through the little vessels (in man's eyes) that are sitting in the church.

While I believe in gathering leaders from within our churches, I also believe sometimes God brings people from outside so that He can pour out His anointing without spilling it all over the place. He has a desire to bring a great blessing, but He has to have structure to capture and distribute it. When He brings leaders in from the outside, it is essential that we teach them how to operate in leadership. We must teach them that their destiny is connected to their leader. They must understand the power of remaining in Godordained attachments. They can't bring offenses they carry from somewhere else and infect our people. They can't bring their own agenda. They must, without exception, speak in these terms: "I am here to help. How can I serve the vision of this church?"

DON'T EXPECT WHAT YOU DON'T INSPECT

Once we've sufficiently trained our leaders, whether they come from within or without, we have to continuously evaluate their progress and performance. In the story of the elite soldiers who arrived to help David, the Bible says that another group that came to fight with David were actually dismissed.[75] It was somewhat like a job application process. David was popular, and men were looking to join his side. Soldiers and warriors kept traveling to find him and ask to be allowed to join David's men. So David had them checked out. He checked their references. He contacted their old employers. And he came across a group that still had a reputation for being loyal to Saul, who was trying to kill David. David inspected their record, and he determined they were not trustworthy. They had an agenda that didn't match his vision.

The Bible says David checked them out. People constantly enter our churches, and no one questions their need to check out the church. They check out the doctrine, the mission, the vision, and the values of the church. And that's right. That's a good thing. As Christians, we should be responsible to understand everything about our Godordained attachments. As much as people are checking out a church, I believe the church should be checking people out. The church leaders should ask the question: "Is this somebody really called to be a part of the house?" Once David was satisfied with the answer yes for the first group of men, he received them, and their hearts were knit together. He was not satisfied with the inspection of the second group, and they were dismissed.

In building the leadership team at the local church, the church leadership must be vigilant in this regard. They cannot allow people to enter and join the team without a season of inspection. It takes more than a single phone call to one reference that the applicant lists on his resume. It takes more than a one-hour interview. In order to build a successful team that lasts, the senior leadership has to research the applicant's background fully.

We cannot expect results that match our vision if we haven't fully inspected the people tasked to implement that vision. David inspected the men who arrived to help him. It was his choice, not the applicants. He was responsible to fully inspect the recruits, and only after a full inspection, make the decision to incorporate them or reject them. This might sound ruthless, but either we are going to lead God's church with fervent diligence, or we might as well do something else. The mission of God is as life-or-death as David's mission in the desert. We must build a team that is up to the task, whose heart is connected, whose attitude is only to help, and whose record passes a detailed inspection for loyalty, excellence, and passion for the church.

"HAVE YOU COME TO HELP?" IN CHURCH LIFE

Years ago, Robin Williams starred in the movie *Mrs. Doubtfire.* At one point in the film, as Robin Williams and his wife were interviewing prospects for a nanny position, one of the applicants began listing all the jobs she wouldn't do. She rattled off, "I don't do dishes. I don't do cooking. I don't walk the dogs." She went on and on, identifying all the things that she simply couldn't be bothered with. It didn't take long for Robin Williams's character's wife to cut her short and politely dismiss her from the interview. This example is over the top, but it makes a clear point. We wouldn't consider hiring someone to care for our children unless they had an attitude to help completely, in whatever area was needed.

Yet I've often seen people come in the church, and they want to come into leadership but only on their terms. They have the area that they are interested in serving—their "ministry"—and they can't be troubled to help out in other areas of church life. They do not understand yet that they are there because the anointing is flowing and they're there to help. Sometimes, you can tell more about a church by who's leaving it than by who's joining. A lady came into our church, and she just saw the church as being able to use the church to fulfill her ministry. She had no real heart or passion to help serve the vision of the house. She had her own vision, her own agenda of what she wanted to do, and she wasn't there to help. She was there to build her personal fan base. She was there to take away from the church rather than bless the church.

Every time we met, she was sure to tell me all about what she could bring to the church. She never asked what the church might need help in. She frequently sought meetings with me to tell me about an idea for Christian Prom Nights. She wanted to have a separate prom night for all the Christian young people. She believed the activity of the students in the public schools, in the "world" if you will, was damaging and a negative influence on the Christian students. While I believe she was properly motivated with a desire to prevent young people from engaging in activities like under-age drinking and promiscuity, she didn't necessarily embrace my philosophy for how to counteract the culture of the world. I completely agree that we should do all we can to help young people make godly decisions in life. While there is legitimacy in her idea, and I want to protect teenagers and guide them toward healthy choices, I believe we are doing our young people a disservice when we simply remove them from the world.

I believe the better answer is to teach, train, and empower our Christian students to be light in darkness. All Christians, regardless of age, are to be the salt of the earth, as Jesus commanded. If we remove all the Christian students from the public school prom nights, we've lost the opportunity to be an example. By isolating our young people, we fail to allow them to be fully used by God to transform and lead culture. God calls us to be separate, not isolated.

In John 17:15-18 Jesus prays for his disciples, "My prayer is not that you take them out of the world but that you protect them from the evil one...As you sent me into the world, I have sent them into the world." Jesus asked God to protect the disciples, and then he sent them into the world to reach the lost.

My vision and message has always been: "Don't curse the darkness, light a candle." In the end, I wasn't opposed to her desire to help young people; I was opposed to her strategy. If we had supported her vision, it would have been contradictory to the very message of our church. It wasn't a part of our church's vision. We are here to reach the lost, not run from them. Ultimately, I believe the better answer is to train our young people to shine in the darkness, not to hide from the world.

After I made it clear that we would not publicly support her idea, she refused to back down. She became subversive and pursued her own agenda, in spite of my instruction.

She showed up at our youth meeting one night with a film crew and told the youth pastor that I had given her my blessing. She shot video, acting as though she was our church's youth pastor, interviewing our young people and creating the impression that I supported what she was doing. In the end, this lady was more interested in what she could get from the church. She was not willing to be under authority; she just desired authority. Jesus Christ loved the church and gave himself for the church. We are called to serve the vision of the church. The church isn't called to serve our vision.

Pastors must always ask the question: "Have you come to help?" when a person introduces a concept for ministry. It may be that God wants the church to take up the cause, but it may just as well be that someone is trying to use the church to build their "platform" and increase their influence.

DEVELOP THE ATTITUDE: I'M HERE TO HELP

1. Have you ever entered a position of leadership without much training? Reflect on your first few months in that position. What could have been done to help you? Are you doing those things to help people you bring into leadership?
2. Does your church have the habit of getting overly excited about a new talented member? Do you value the "sons and daughters of the house"? Is there a balance between leaders from within and without on your team?

3. Do you ever complain when asked to do something outside of your department? Is your attitude reflective of a heart that will do whatever it takes to help?
4. Do you take the time to review and inspect the attitudes and work product of the people you lead? If they are sub-par, are you training them instead of blaming them?

A SPIRIT OF EXCELLENCE

Oh Lord, our Lord, how excellent is Your name in all the earth!

Psalm 8:1

A spirit of excellence maintains its appetite for greatness, regardless of current circumstances. A spirit of excellence helps us remain awake to the details. A person with a spirit of excellence is a participator in life, never a mere spectator. The spirit of excellence drives a person to overcome insecurities, to be punctual, and to pursue improvement in all things. When we live with a spirit of excellence, we best reflect God and honor His great name!

If you are going to achieve excellence in big things, you develop the habit in little matters. Excellence is not an exception but a prevailing attitude.

—General Colin Powell

A SPIRIT OF EXCELLENCE MAINTAINS
ITS APPETITE FOR GREATNESS

Our God is excellent. All that He does is excellent. He demonstrated His spirit of excellence when He gave instructions to Noah to build the ark. He provided Noah with precise dimensions and materials. He designed an excellent ship that would preserve the human race.[76]

God further manifested his spirit of excellence when He told Solomon how to build the temple. God wanted to build a house for Himself that was great and would reflect His spirit of excellence. The construction of God's house took seven years. It was funded in part by a contribution of two hundred million dollars, in modern valuation, from David and his inner leadership!

Clearly God spared no expense in the construction and the details of His house! The house of God, the Church, should have a spirit of excellence. It should reflect the majesty and wonder of God. Yet, over and over again, I hear people ask, "Why are we spending all this money on a church building?" And others will be very direct and ask me, "What are the costs to build Wave Church? How much did all this lighting and sound equipment cost?" My response always is, "Nowhere near as much as what God required and what God spent to build His house in the Old Testament."

Our church goal is not to build big buildings for my ego. Our church goal is to design and build facilities that honor the excellence of our God and draw people to His goodness and love. Every seat in our building represents a life that could be saved. Every element of lighting, sound, and design is created to invite people into the presence of God Almighty. Quite simply, the building of the house of God is about people, people He created. Our God is an excellent God, and we need to maintain an appetite for excellence.

After all, God made trees with fruit that was both "pleasing to the eye *and* good for food" (emphasis added).[77] God desires beauty and function. He created all things with aesthetic appeal and practical use.

From time to time, however, even the most excellent spirit has to chew on some mediocrity. We've got to learn to keep our appetite for excellence. When I first arrived in Virginia Beach, I had a vision for excellence, but it would be years before that vision became reality. And today, I have vision beyond where we are! During my earliest years in Virginia, we used an overhead projector for our worship displays. Inside I was hungering for a big screen with multimedia capabilities, but I remained patient. I chewed on the mediocrity, but I never developed the appetite for anything but excellence. Though I had to wait, I refused to accept mediocre as the standard for our church.

Of course, if you walk into our building today, it's state of the art. Our convention center has been given architectural design awards. We've had local dignitaries call our building "A jewel of the city." I believe this honors God and demonstrates the excellence of His nature. No one noticed or commented during the days before the buildings were completed, "I believe in architectural evangelism." The construction of the buildings brought people to see the excellence who never would have visited otherwise. During the five to seven years before our newest buildings were opened, there were many services and moments where I had to accept that we weren't yet as excellent as I desired. I remember chewing on some mediocrity, but I always had an appetite for excellence.

Our children's facility is one of the best public buildings up and down the East Coast of America. In 2005, it received The Hampton Roads Association for Commercial Real Estate Excellence in Development Design Award—Best Public Building. It houses a Montessori preschool, a daycare program, and a before-andafter school program. Before we built our children's facility, I guess people had not fully realized the appetite that I had for excellence. When they saw it and they walked through it, they wept and were overwhelmed by its beauty. They were astonished by the details. In the area of technology alone, we have monitors that webcast so parents can see their children online during the day.

This element alone is an outworking of an excellent spirit. We are located in Hampton Roads, which has the largest navy base in the world, and we have a lot of military parents with children in our programs. While they are faithfully serving our country overseas, they're able to get online and see their children through the online cameras, which are secured and encrypted. We have biometric technology for our daycare program and for our student check-in during our Sunday services. This equipment operates by having parents put their finger on a fingerprint computer system that is catalogued with a photo of their child, so our children's ministry workers never give the wrong child to the wrong guardian.

In my opinion, we cannot build the house of God to be anything less than excellent. We must be willing to be patient; we must not get overly burdened with debt. But we cannot allow temporary mediocre moments to become our accepted fare. We may have to manage for a season by chewing on mediocrity, but we must always maintain our spirit of excellence.

As a practical example, at Wave Church in the past 12 years we have been able to grow but keep a sharp eye on our debts. We work hard to save expenses and preserve the great assets God has provided. We have fully paid the debt owed for thirty-one acres of land on our south property. We're debt free for the land costs on our twenty-one acres at our main campus. We've paid off the entire four million dollar construction loan of the 30,000-square-foot children's facility that we completed in 2004.

At our main campus, the construction of Wave Convention Center was completed in 2008. The City of Virginia Beach Planning Commission awarded us with an Outstanding Private Institutional Design Merit Award. This facility is over 120,000 square feet and includes our main auditorium, which seats 2,500 people, as well as pastoral offices, classroom space for our children's ministry, and our Wave Leadership College classrooms, offices, and library. In 2010, we were able to pay 1.3 million dollars in cash for a significant parking expansion. In 2012, we opened our newest campus, a 4.4 million dollar, five-hundred-seat auditorium with daycare facility, classrooms, offices, etc. It is a beautiful example to the community. It also has a T1 line to simulcast services, and as of this book's writing, we are almost completely debt free on this construction. All of this is to invite more people to come and see hear of our amazing, excellent God!

A SPIRIT OF EXCELLENCE STAYS AWAKE TO THE DETAILS

We have excellent, stateoftheart facilities. We had to chew on some mediocrity for a long time. And though we've seen great buildings built, we're not finished. We're just getting started. The projects may be complete, but a spirit of excellence stays awake to the details of ongoing improvement. Even now in our building I feel like we have to be so careful that we don't become laissez-faire. We can't get sloppy or think that we've "arrived" because the buildings are completed. We can't begin to compare our facilities to other churches' buildings.

Too often, we only look at size or cost as a measure of excellence. I think somebody can actually have a facility that costs less and is smaller, but they can be be more excellent than what we are because they are doing the best with what they have been given. If my church doesn't keep its spirit of excellence, if we fall asleep or become lazy, if we tolerate mediocrity, we are in danger.

By comparison, our church might still look excellent to others, but the truth is we aren't achieving excellence with what we have been called to be. Excellence is not about being the best. It's about doing the best with what you have.

There is a difference between a spirit of excellence and a moment of excellence. Anyone can experience a moment of excellence. It takes sustained effort, discipline, and passion to keep a spirit of excellence. The Bible teaches that slothfulness casts a person into a deep sleep.[78] This is a wake-up call. If you become accustomed to mediocre, to "near enough is good enough," you will find yourself in a comatose state. You will be ineffective, disoriented, and lacking excellence. Wake up!

If you're not faithful in the little things, then God can never give you more.[79] We have to be careful in our attitude toward our facilities. Though everything looks excellent, we have to be careful that slothfulness doesn't cast us into a deep sleep. In our church administration, we have to remain as diligent and fervent for helping people as we were the first day our doors opened. The moment we begin to put things off, that's the moment we begin to lose momentum and we begin to slip toward mediocrity. Abraham Lincoln said, "Never put off to tomorrow what can be done today."

Of course, I can be as guilty of procrastination as anyone else. I think about a time back in Australia when I was heading up the Bible college. I invited a pastor friend to come speak in the Bible college for us, and he stayed as a guest in our home the night before speaking. We had a great dinner, chatted about life, and then I showed him to our guest bedroom/bathroom and said goodnight.

Our guest bedroom and bathroom were rarely occupied. Every once in a while, when I was in that part of the house, I noticed that the doorknob was getting looser on the bathroom door. I always thought to myself "I need to fix that," but I never got around to it. The doorknob got looser, and finally the doorknob fell off. I put off re-attaching the doorknob and eventually we didn't even know where the doorknob was anymore, and there was now just the hole in the door where the doorknob should have been. But I never worried about it. It was out of sight and out of mind. It didn't really affect us. For months, I'd stroll by and remember but as soon as I walked away, I forgot to repair it once again.

The morning my friend was to speak in the college, Sharon and I both had to leave early. He had his own car, so I left him to drive himself to the college. He was due to speak at 10:00 a.m. About 9:45, I went to the front of the building to await his arrival. He wasn't there. The clock ticked. Five minutes, ten minutes passed. He still had not arrived. It was 10:10, and there was no sign of him. I began to fear that he'd been in a car accident. I told the students to review for their next class, and I left to go find him.

I didn't see anything on the roads that led me to think he'd been in an accident. *Maybe he got lost?* I thought. I arrived at my house and called out for him. I heard a faint reply. I followed his voice back to the guest room, and to my absolute horror, he was locked in our bathroom. He had showered, had nothing on but a towel, and was trapped in our bathroom!

When he shut the door, the internal mechanism had locked the door, and he couldn't get out. He had tried fiddling with it with a toothbrush handle, he had even stuck a few Q-tips in there, but he was stuck! All because I was slothful and had fallen asleep to the need to repair the problem. If I had tightened the doorknob the first time I noticed it was loose, it would have taken me a minute, and the door would have operated normally. Now, because of my procrastination, the entire college schedule was disrupted for hundreds of students, my friend was inconvenienced, and I was humiliated. I often share this story with my church as a way of reinforcing how critical it is that we keep our spirit of excellence by staying awake to the details.

One of the ways to check yourself in this area is to walk around your house as though you were preparing for someone you really respect to visit. Suddenly, you'll notice all the things that you have been putting off. You'll see marks on the walls, stains on the carpets, maybe a piece of broken furniture. You once noticed these things, but you've fallen into a "deep sleep." Until someone you really respect is going to come and visit your house, then all of a sudden you notice those things because you're awake, you're looking at it through the eyes of the person that's visiting your house.

Maybe it's not your home but your car that needs a "fresh eyes" inspection. Again, it's not about having the best car in the world; it's about taking care of what you have. Maybe the fuel gauge doesn't work, and you just keep driving it and thinking about fixing it, but you don't do anything to fix it. Then, one day when you're driving with someone you want to make a good impression on, you run out of gas. Now you're embarrassed that you ran out of gas, and it was all because you didn't stay awake to the details. Having a spirit of excellence means that you are not only engaged in the big moments, but you stay awake to the importance of small details.

A SPIRIT OF EXCELLENCE IS A PARTICIPATOR, NOT A SPECTATOR

In Psalm 103:7 we read of God, "He made known His ways to Moses, and His acts unto the children of Israel." This is a fascinating verse. It demonstrates the full intimacy that Moses had with God. It also reveals the viewpoint the Israelites had of God. The children of Israel saw God turn the river in Egypt into blood. The children of Israel saw God bring locusts and frogs and plagues into Egypt. The children of Israel saw the Angel of Death sweep over Egypt and kill all the first-born sons except for those who had the blood marked on the doorposts of their home. The children of Israel saw God take them, with Moses, through the Red Sea.

The children of Israel saw God every day supernaturally feed them with manna from heaven. The children of Israel saw the cloud of God by day protecting them from the heat of the desert and the pillar of fire keeping them warm every night. The children of Israel experienced the power of God supernaturally, for over forty years, keeping as new their clothing and their shoes. The children of Israel saw water flow out of a rock.

The children of Israel saw some amazing things! Even one of those things would be mind-blowing to witness. The Israelites saw the outward expressions of God's supreme power. But Moses was able to know God's ways. I don't know about you, but I'd love to be the kind of person who doesn't just see the miracles of God, but understands why God does them.

I don't want to just be a spectator. I want to be a participator. I want to be a part of what God is doing. I want to be so excellent that God accomplishes His work through me. If the children of Israel spoke modern English, they probably would have commented when God made water rush forth from a rock, "That's cool. I wonder how God did that?"

Moses was able to say, "I know how he did it. I can make that happen again." Are we spectators or participators? The Israelites were spectators. They could see excellent things. But it takes more than witnessing excellence to have a spirit of excellence. Having a spirit of excellence requires participating in excellent works.

I have an assistant who helps me with a multiplicity of personal needs. He takes care of my car, and he takes care of my lawn, for example. He's a great blessing to Sharon and I and very much involved in our personal lives. His work for us enables us to pursue excellence for God, in our family life, and in our church ministry and traveling ministry. He has a tough job. I'm a fussy person. For example, I have certain requirements for the maintenance and operation of my car. I want my car prepared every weekend with a full tank of gas so I don't have to worry about running out of gas on the weekend as I'm getting to and from the different church campuses. When I speak at our main campus, the cameras project my image onto a sixty-five-foot wide screen. The car needs to be clean so if I happen to brush up against it in my suit, I'm not going to have dirt on me, which would be revealed very vividly on that screen. These are just a couple simple examples of the attention to detail that is necessary so that we can be as effective as possible, with a spirit of excellence, in building the church.

I hold him to a high standard. Over time he's been able to meet the standard. He can perform acts of excellence because he's being managed by me. There's a template that's been given to him. He's following directions. It's become standard operating procedure. But just because he can do acts with excellence doesn't mean he has internalized a spirit of excellence.

The act of excellence is doing what you've been told well, but the spirit of excellence isn't just what you do to get paid or receive a reward. The spirit of excellence is a way of life. Just because you can clean my car well doesn't guarantee that you keep your car neat. There is a distinction between doing and observing excellence and carrying a spirit of excellence. Moses carried a spirit of excellence, which was given to him by God. If you've been spending most of your time as a spectator, ask God to help you become a participator in works of excellence. If you are a participator, don't think too highly of yourself. Stay humble and hungry, and keep pursuing everything with a spirit of excellence.

A SPIRIT OF EXCELLENCE IS PUNCTUAL

Just as there is a great difference between seeing the acts of God and knowing His ways, there is a big difference between seeing a photograph and watching a movie. A photograph is a moment captured in time. It is a still shot, an isolated, frozen moment. A movie is a long, continuously active sequence of images that form a more layered story than we could every draw from simply looking at a picture. If you were to take one image from a movie, you couldn't appreciate the story because you'd have no context. Our lives have context. They are more than a momentary snapshot. They are an ever-unfolding complex story of decisions and interactions. Over time, however, a recurring image or characteristic is likely to appear. One recurring image of those who have a spirit of excellence is punctuality.

Our church has staff meetings every week, and I expect our staff to be there on time, to have that spirit of excellence. If one of the staff members is late, and they apologize, they will be forgiven. Perhaps there was a legitimate reason for being tardy. If it happens once every two or three years, that's understandable. The day they were late is a photograph, but the movie of their life tells a different story. The movie of their life is one of excellence and punctuality. If, on the other hand, the movie turns out to be one of perpetual tardiness, then there's a deeper problem than just setting an alarm clock. They are lacking a spirit of excellence, and that is unacceptable.

One of the interesting things about perpetually late people is the excuses. If I weren't so passionate about excellence, I would find it entertaining to listen to their stories. They are clever and creative in their defense for being late. The book of Proverbs has many illustrations for this propensity. One of my favorites is, "The sluggard is wiser in his own eyes than seven men that can render a reason."[80]

Having a lifestyle lacking in punctuality is disrespectful to others. If you're always late, you actually are saying to people, "My time is more valuable than yours." Your attitude projects, "No one is telling me where to be when. I'm doing what I want when I want." I actually think that's a very controlling spirit, and it shows great dishonor. If you are fifteen minutes late for a meeting and there are ten people sitting there waiting for you to arrive so the meeting can start, well, then your fifteen minutes may not mean much to you, but that's 150 minutes of those other people's productive time that was wasted sitting around waiting for you to arrive. I believe a spirit of excellence respects other people by respecting their time.

A SPIRIT OF EXCELLENCE OVERCOMES INSECURITY

A spirit of excellence is secure. It doesn't think about the critics' comments. Maybe somebody will say something negative or critical about you. The spirit of excellence doesn't respond in kind. The spirit of excellence lives above the critic's voice. Jesus lived above his critics.

I realize that we're all human beings, and we all have feelings, but I believe when you have a spirit of excellence, you have tremendous security. A person with a spirit of excellence does not look down on people, either. A spirit of excellence does not carry a sense of entitlement or elitism. A man or woman with a spirit of excellence realizes that his or her life can be a model, an example to others. So long as they remain humble before God, their example will be a powerful force for God. They will inspire others by remaining committed to excellence in spite of the voices of the critic.

Maybe the critic that you have to overcome isn't a family member or an enemy, or a former teacher or coach. The critic that you have to overcome is the one who looks back at you in the mirror every day. The hardest critic is often oneself. You face insecurities that no one else even knows about. But with the spirit of excellence you can and will become secure.

Once again, I turn to Moses as an example of a great leader who faced internal challenges. In this case, it was Moses's insecurity about his own abilities. Moses, like many of us, was his own worst critic! In Exodus 3-4, we read of the interaction between God and Moses as God called Moses to rescue the Israelites.

When God first approached Moses in the wilderness, He spoke to him through a burning bush. God said, "Moses, I want you to go tell Pharaoh to let my people go." Moses promptly began giving excuses, based on his insecurities. "I can't do it. I can't speak properly."

So God obliges Moses and begins showing demonstrations of His power to put Moses at ease. He has

Moses put his hand in his coat, and when he pulled it out, it had leprosy, and then when he put it back again, he was healed. And then Moses put down his staff, and it turned into a snake, and then God said, "Pick it up again," and it was a rod again. God was doing everything He could to accommodate Moses's arguments and insecurity.

And then finally, when Moses said, "Look, I just can't speak properly, send somebody else," God said, "Here comes Aaron. Let him speak for you." Just prior to God allowing Aaron to participate in leadership with Moses, Exodus 4:14 reads, "And the anger of God was kindled against Moses." God was frustrated with Moses's insecurity! Moses's lack of security was so debilitating that even after God displayed extraordinary power through Moses's own body, he still didn't trust God to speak through him!

This passage shows us that it was actually Moses's insecurity that gave Aaron a position of leadership. Aaron was not necessary. If Moses—after the first or second miracle—had realized how secure He was in God, God would have never summoned Aaron. If Moses had a clue about the spirit of excellence that God had placed in him, he would have said, "Yes, Lord," and started marching to Egypt. Instead, God had to keep working with Moses's insecurity. And God did not want Aaron to do it; He wanted Moses to do it. But the lack of a spirit of excellence, and the insecurity it bred in Moses, compelled God to add Aaron to the team.

Aaron, as the second in command, had great authority with the people. He was given a platform because Moses didn't initially operate with a spirit of excellence. Because of Moses's insecurity and lack of faith in God, Aaron became a spokesperson. When Moses went up onto the mountain to be with God and receive the commandments, the people approached Aaron. They said, "Aaron, we don't know where Moses is. He's been gone a few weeks. Now you do something. You lead us."[81] And Aaron didn't know what to do, and the people all got together with Aaron and determined that the best thing to do was to build an idol to worship! They brought their gold earrings to Aaron, and he melted the jewelry and turned it into a golden calf. The people began sacrificing to the golden calf, which caused God to interrupt His meeting with Moses.

God yells at Moses and tells him to go down and see what the Israelites are doing. God then tells Moses that He will destroy them and make Moses a great nation. Moses pleads with God not to destroy the Israelites, and God relents.[82] And, of course, when Moses came down from the mountain, he saw what the people did, and he was so angry.

Later, Moses confronts Aaron, and the Bible says, "Aaron had not restrained the people, to the shame of their enemies."[83] Aaron was never meant to be a leader. In the moment of crisis, he did not restrain or lead the people. He gave into their demands and failed to hold them accountable to the commands of God. This entire debacle of idol worship can be traced to Moses's own insecurity, which provided Aaron with the opportunity to be a leader.

We must not be insecure in our calling. Have a spirit of excellence that believes God to provide for your weaknesses. If you don't, you may end up in the same position as Moses, having to clean up the mess made by someone who never should have been leading in the first place.

A SPIRIT OF EXCELLENCE IN CHURCH LIFE

When I first arrived in Virginia Beach, the building that served as our auditorium had plenty of areas for improvement. The biggest problem was that it was never designed to be an auditorium for church services. It had been part of a comprehensive building program and was intended to be the children's church area and administrative offices. Unfortunately, the church never finished the building program, and as a result, used an awkward, open, flat space for its services.

This space had support beams throughout, which provided plenty of line-of-sight difficulties. The flat floor made it difficult for people toward the back of the building to see over the heads of the people in front of them. The power was insufficient. If the air conditioning was running in the summer, and we plugged in multiple coffee pots in our lobby, we invariably blew a fuse. This building presented plenty of challenges, and I had to manage internal frustrations in order for us to keep pushing forward. Of all the problems this building presented, none was more awkward and difficult as the location of the bathrooms.

The only public restrooms in the auditorium—the ones that anyone in a service would use if they needed to—were located directly to the left and right of the stage. During the service, with everyone looking directly at the stage, if a person needed to go to the restroom, they literally walked down the outside of the seats, as everyone still seated had his or her attention diverted to watch them walk to the bathroom! Talk about a going problem! It was a major distraction during a service. Imagine trying to preach, and trying to keep the congregation's attention, when every five minutes or so someone comes strolling down the aisle and heads to your right or left to use the bathroom. But I couldn't relocate the restrooms. So I had to chew on the mediocrity, but we were good stewards. We kept the bathrooms nice and clean and made the best of it.

After Sharon and I had been there for a couple years and we had begun to experience positive momentum, I spoke to the church about a desire to invest in some small renovations in the building. The carpet, for one, was the original carpet that had been installed almost twenty years earlier. When I first presented the idea of spending to improve the facilities, some people resisted. They knew—as did I—that we were planning on eventually demolishing the building and constructing a new facility. But a spirit of excellence does not sacrifice the immediate for some far-off event. The spirit of excellence works with diligence to make every moment the best it can be.

I explained to the people that we get one shot at making a good impression. When people walk through our doors, we have mere moments to present our best for the Lord and win them to His cause. Part of this effort is being excellent in all that we do. Because our church is dedicated to saving the lost, we decided to spend money on the lobby—because that's the first impression new people have of our church. I remember one of our key leaders and businessmen asked, "What's wrong with the foyer?" He wasn't asking with a mean spirit—he was supportive and participated. But he simply could not see the need to upgrade the foyer. He didn't yet have a vision for the kind of excellence that I was pursuing for our church.

The renovation went very well. We put in a café style coffee bar, we replaced the carpet with nice tiling, we put some better lighting in, and we put some small TV screens on the wall. Essentially, we created a space where people would like to hang out. I wanted a place where people could relax after a service and make new friends, not just race out the door because there was nothing happening. This area gave them an opportunity to linger and fellowship and build connections with each other.

After the first few weeks, that same leader who questioned the decision to upgrade the lobby approached me. "I can't believe I asked you that question," he said. "It wasn't until I saw what you did that I realized how I had become used to mediocrity and I was asleep to just how good things could be. Now I see what your appetite for excellence is, and all I can say is, I want more."

I loved when he said that, because I knew we had reached a turning point in our expectations for excellence. The leaders had hung in there with me during the early days when we didn't have the resources to build what we wanted. Now the initial results of a spirit of excellence were starting to show, and it just inspired us all to dream bigger. When you are building God's church, remember to be a good steward of what he has entrusted to you, but never compromise excellence in the name of saving a few dollars. He's God of the universe; he deserves the most excellent house we can build.

DEVELOP A SPIRIT OF EXCELLENCE

1. Do you have areas in your life that are not as excellent as you desire? Have you lived with mediocrity for so long that you've lost your appetite for excellence?

2. Are you awake to the details? Have you done a "fresh eyes" inspection of your home or your car recently? How about your closet? Are you excellent in only the areas that other people see?

3. Are you a participator or a spectator? Do you give of yourself to make others more excellent? Are you driven to make things excellent the first time, or do you wait for someone else to clean up your mess?

4. Are you punctual? Are you secure that God will use you in the areas where He's called you? Do you recognize how excellent He is and the importance of representing Him well to the world?

THE POWER OF A GOOD REPORT

Whatever things are of good report…meditate on these things.

Philippians 4:8

You get one life. That life is created by your speech, and your thoughts create your speech. Think on good things. Seeking and speaking the best about your situation will only improve your situation. Life is a mirror: what you project is reflected back by society. Develop the habit of giving a good report. In this way, you will improve the world around you, your life will bear fruit, and you will honor God by wearing Him well.

Let us go up at once and take possession, for we are well able to overcome them.

—Caleb

YOUR LIFE IS CREATED BY YOUR SPEECH; YOUR SPEECH IS CREATED BY YOUR THOUGHTS

There is an ongoing struggle for your decisions. God tells us to think good thoughts. He encourages us to speak by faith. Our natural bias is downward. Who wins in this struggle will determine whether or not your life is as positive as the dreams of a new mother, or as dismal as the first five minutes of the evening news. What we think determines what we say. What we say determines how we influence the world around us and within us. Speak a good report.

Meditating on a good report is more than simply being positive about life's circumstances. It is not merely being a "glass half full" kind of person. Meditating on a good report places our focus on the best and most noble parts of life.[84]Giving a good report follows this thinking and is the only way we can build God's house, because the essence of faith is the ability to give a good report.

I often remark, "Some people are so negative that if you put them in a darkroom, they develop." I joke, but only slightly. The truth is fear is the darkroom where we develop all of our negatives. I ask some people, "How are you doing?" And they reply, "Not too bad." I always think, what kind of an answer is "not too bad"? If you're not too bad, why don't you say, "I'm bordering on good"? I'll ask a guy, "How's work going?" and he'll reply, "I'm just making a living—it's paying the bills." While I realize that there are tough times, if we could speak from a more positive aspect, I think we'd be surprised at how far it takes us—above and beyond our immediate fears.

Proverbs 23:7 explains, "As a man thinks in his heart, so is he." In other words, we become what we think about. Your current reality is not determined by your environment, your socioeconomic background, or your educational experience. If you come from a bad home, it doesn't mean you need to have a bad life. If you really want to know the future, you don't need to visit a clairvoyant or a mystical person who can go into the spirit realm and talk to some deceased ancestor. You don't need a prophet, a prophetess, or even a word of knowledge. To know the future, all you need to do is understand that scripture. As a man thinks in his heart, so is he.

God tells us to think on "whatever is true, whatever is right, whatever is pure, whatever is lovely, whatever is admirable."[85] He teaches us to do this because He knows that we are the product of our thought lives. When we think on good things, we do good things.

If this is a challenge for you, try actively speaking positive things about the future and the people in your life. Romans 10:9 reads, "If you *confess with your mouth* the Lord Jesus and *believe in your heart* that God has raised Him from the dead…" (emphasis added). Confession precedes belief. By making the declaration that Jesus is the Savior, we create the future belief in our heart for that reality. When we speak, we control our beliefs.

Try speaking only positively about your spouse for a week. Try speaking only nice things about your boss for a day. If you find yourself struggling, or if you find yourself unable to say anything, you are someone who needs to develop the ability to speak a good report. Remember, you are creating your life's future by how you speak. Think about what you're saying, and only speak what you want to believe.

SEEKING AND SPEAKING THE BEST WILL ONLY IMPROVES YOUR SITUATION

It's hard to overstate the power of a good report. A situation can be perceived as an improvement opportunity or an insurmountable obstacle—it's all about how we speak and believe. A big part of perception framing and forming is the words we choose. Leadership is all about managing people's perceptions. It's about leading people's thinking, leading people's thoughts. If you can lead a thought, you can lead your life, as well as others. If you can lead your life, you can improve your life. You can change your life for the better into all that God has for it if you can just learn to control your thoughts. As a man thinks in his heart, so is he.[86]

The creation account in Genesis 1-2 is a powerful illustration of the importance of a good report. The Bible says that in the beginning the earth was formless and void, and there was darkness. So God said, "Let there be light." And there was light. Just imagine if God just reported what he saw. What if God had said, "Boy, it sure is dark out there!"? There would have just been more darkness. God created the world that He lived in with the words that He spoke. You and I will create the world we live in with our words. We are made in the image and likeness of God. God made the world, but He let Adam name the animals that populated his world. God lets us name the actions that populate our world. We have the power to speak life or death by our report—will we speak good or ill?

For example, if you say to your wife, "You'll never change," how do you expect her to improve? If you say to your children, "You're hopeless," how can you believe for them to have a positive attitude? You are framing your world, and you are sentencing them to less than great in life by your words. The words you choose have a source. Jesus said, "Out of the abundance of the heart the mouth speaks."[87] The words coming out of your mouth flow from your heart. In order to speak more positively about your wife, your children, your boss, you must improve the condition of your heart. In order to improve your heart, you must first have a relationship with Jesus Christ, and you must keep your perspective focused on the good things in life. It's easy to point out the problems in life. God could have done that at the beginning of time. He chose to speak the best about His situation. Because of His choice, we exist. Choose to speak and seek the best in your situations—it certainly won't make things worse; in fact, it may be the only thing that can make things better.

LIFE IS A MIRROR; SOCIETY REFLECTS YOUR PERCEPTIONS

I genuinely believe life is a mirror. Your family, community, and society will only reflect back to you how you perceive yourself. If you want to change the way other people see you, you've got to change the way you see yourself. It starts with understanding the power of a good report. It starts with keeping a positive perspective and outlook on life. It starts by viewing a challenging proposition from a higher perspective: a God perspective.

Even in the body of Christ, most people will choose to view things from a negative perspective. The story of the twelve Israelite spies provides great evidence of this bias. In Exodus 13, God announces to Moses that He's ready to give the Israelites the Promised Land.[88] He asked Moses to gather twelve elite men from the tribes of Israel. Moses recruited the heads of the tribes. These were top-notch men. These were the leaders. Of anyone in the nation of Israel, these men should be the most positive people. Moses told them to take the high road. He told them to view the land of Canaan from the mountains.[89]

In other words, he encouraged them to get a perspective from above rather than from below. He wanted them to have a view from the top—to see the world as God sees it. So they begin going the way Moses told them, according to Exodus 13:22. Then the course diverged from the high places. "Then they came to the valley of Eshcol and they cut down a branch with one cluster of grapes; they carried it on a pole between two men."[90] They went down into the valley and began to allow fear to creep in. They got close to the enemy, and they saw the size of the fruit. They wanted to bring back proof to the Israelites—not of how amazingly fertile the land was, but of how large the challenge was before them!

When they finished their mission, the ten negative spies were explaining the giants in the promise land and declared, "We were as grasshoppers in our own eyes, and so we were in their eyes."[91] Those ten spies brought back a negative report, and all of the children of Israel believed the negative report rather than the positive report. Joshua and Caleb said, "They're but bread for us. We can surely go in, and we can possess the land."[92]

Because of the perspective of the ten weak spies, the Israelites were condemned to wander in the wilderness until everyone of that leadership generation died. The only two people from that generation that went in to possess the land was Joshua and Caleb. God punished Israel because they believed the negativity of the ten spies.

The perspective of those ten spies ruined the opportunity for millions to experience God's promised blessing. How many people are you limiting by your negative perspective? God wants to use you to do greater things, but perhaps your negative self-perceptions and comparisons of yourself to others have limited your ability to speak a good report.

This truth is not just about people's perceptions. It includes genuine pains and wrongs that people carry with them into new relationships. People who come from damaged backgrounds, people who have been hurt do have to work extra hard to be positive. It is a true statement to say that *hurting people hurt people*. If you are a hurting person, daily choose to give that hurt to Jesus and focus on the good things in your world.

Another true saying is: people don't see things the way they really are; they see things the way *they* are. If you see yourself as negative and defeated, then that's how you'll see the world, whether the world is like that or not. Negativity will become your reality, and life will only reflect negativity back to you, even though the true reality is not as bad as your perceptions.

Have you ever noticed that positive people always end up hanging around positive, happy people? Have you also noticed that negative people always end up hanging around negative people? Before I was a Christian, when I was drinking copious amounts of alcohol and experimenting with drugs, it was almost magnetic how I would find somebody who was doing drugs. No matter where I went; they'd find me, or I'd find them. Now, having been a Christian for thirty years, I never seem to run into those people. Why? Because life is a mirror. Life only reflects back to you what's in you. The following story illustrates this principle to perfection:

> Two brothers once decided to leave their hometown and move to the city. Outside the city the first brother met an old man.
>
> "How are the people here?" asked the first brother.
>
> "Well, how were the people in your hometown?" asked the old man in return.
>
> "Aw, they were always grumpy and dissatisfied," answered the first brother. "There wasn't a single one among them worth bothering about."
>
> "And," the old man said, "you'll find that the people here are exactly the same!"

A little while later the other brother came along.

"How are the people in this city?" he asked.

"How were the people in your hometown?" the old man asked as before.

"Fine!" said the other brother. "Always cheerful, always kind and understanding!"

"You will find that the people her are exactly the same!" said the old man again, for he was a wise old man who knew that the attitude of the people you meet depends upon your own state of mind. [93]

If you are cheerful and frank and good-humored, you'll find others the same.

THOSE THAT GIVE A GOOD REPORT WILL BEAR FRUIT

Just as the brothers in that story demonstrate, the way we describe the world around us determines how we perceive life. The Bible describes men as having "fruit of the lips," which is the words we speak. [94] By our words we bear fruit, which becomes our life's nourishment. [95] When Jesus was tempted by Satan after forty days in the wilderness, He told the devil, "Man does not live by bread alone, but by every Word that proceeds from the mouth of God." [96]

Since words are fruit and provide nourishment, it naturally follows that a good report will bear good fruit. This is a significant point. Bearing fruit is the singular defining characteristic of those who are believers in Christ.

John 15:1-17 says (emphasis added):

> I am the true vine, and My Father is the vine-dresser. Every branch in Me that does not bear fruit He takes away; and every *branch* that bears fruit He prunes, that it may bear more fruit. You are already clean because of the word that I have spoken to you. Abide in Me, and I in you. As the branch cannot bear fruit of itself, unless it abides in the vine, neither can you, unless you abide in Me. "I am the vine, you *are* the branches. He who abides in Me, and I in him, bears much fruit; for without Me you can do nothing. If anyone does not abide in Me, he is cast out as a branch and is withered; and men gather them and throw *them* into the fire, and they are burned.
>
> If you abide in Me, and My words abide in you, you will ask what you desire, and it shall be done for you. By this My Father is glorified, that you bear much fruit; so you will be My disciples. As the Father loved Me, I also have loved you; abide in My love. If you keep My commandments, you will abide in My love, just as I have kept My Father's commandments and abide in His love.
>
> These things I have spoken to you, that My joy may remain in you, and *that* your joy may be full. This is My commandment, that you love one another as I have loved you. Greater love has no one than this, than to lay down one's life for his friends. You are My friends if you

do whatever I command you. No longer do I call you servants, for a servant does not know what his master is doing; but I have called you friends, for all things that I heard from My Father I have made known to you. You did not choose Me, but I chose you and appointed you that you should go and bear fruit, and *that* your fruit should remain, that whatever you ask the Father in My name He may give you. These things I command you, that you love one another.

There are two types of branches mentioned in verses 5-6 of this passage. The first is the branch that abides in Christ and bears much fruit. The second is the branch that does not abide in Christ and does not bear fruit. This branch is cast out or cut off from the tree. Men gather these branches and throw them in the fire to be burned. You get to choose which branch you are going to be. If you want to be a fruit-bearing branch, a part of that choice is giving a good report, because giving a good report will bear fruit. In verse 2, Jesus says that the fruit-bearing branches will be pruned, but the barren branches will be completely cut off. Either way, there are blades involved! You choose, by abiding in Him and having a good report, to be a branch that is trimmed rather than completely severed from the vine.

Jesus explains that the branch that doesn't bear fruit, that doesn't abide in Him, is "cast forth," or tossed out. These are people in the church who end up feeling out of it, they feel isolated, and they don't feel like they're in step with everybody else. They are cast forth and begin to act withdrawn and isolated. They begin to say things like, "The church has changed. It's not the same. It's not what it used to be. It's not friendly. The church has grown, and it's become unfriendly." Earlier in this chapter I made the point that people don't see things the way they really are, they see things the way *they* are. This happens to the branches that are cast forth. There's a casting forth that happens when a person is not abiding in Christ—when they don't have the spirit of faith and they aren't bearing fruit because they don't have a good report.

It's not easy to be one of these branches. After being cast out, Jesus says they are "withered." They become bitter, critical, judgmental, and disheveled. Their spirit dries up. They've lost connection to the vine, the source of life. They've lost the spirit of faith. They have lost the spirit of optimism. They no longer believe in the possibilities of breakthrough and hope. They've become a victim rather than a victor. And they become more comfortable in that environment than they are in an environment of good reports and positive attitudes.

Unfortunately, it gets worse for these branches. In verse 6, Jesus says that men gather the branches that have been cast out and are now withered. It's a spiritual principle that these branches end up "collecting" each other. After a while, the "cast out" branches begin to meet others with the same report. They talk and discover a similarity. They express to each other, "Do you feel like people just don't understand how hard things are? Oh, I'm so glad you feel that way. That's exactly how I feel." These people begin to build an isolated world with their negative reports to one another.

After they've found each other and been gathered, verse 6 says they are thrown into fire and are burned. This is the most tragic part of the analogy that Jesus makes between branches and people. The second set of branches are people that become so completely cut off from the source of truth and the power of a good report, they don't even smell the smoke as they approach the fire. They are simply bundled up with those in a similar state and are cast into destruction. The worst part is that they can end up causing harm and damage to the church and to other people who join in their negativity.

We are all branches, and we are all susceptible to becoming the second type of branch. No one wants to be a cast-off branch. It happens slowly if we allow ourselves to project a negative report that yields no fruit. We can choose to be the type of branch that is merely pruned, abides in Him, and bears fruit. It all depends on our commitment to bringing a good report.

WHEN WE GIVE A GOOD REPORT, WE HONOR GOD AND WEAR HIM WELL

By now, you understand the importance of a good report as it relates to your own blessing and success. It is important to internalize this principle and live by it every day. Of greater importance is understanding that when we give a good report, we honor God.

Hebrews 13:15 tells us, "let us offer the sacrifice of praise to God continually, that is, the fruit of our lips." Again, the expression "fruit of our lips" is used in the context of a tangible creation. We are making a sacrifice when we praise God. How is praise a sacrifice?

Praise becomes a sacrifice when it's done in the midst of troubling times. It's easy to give thanks when you've just received a miracle. The sacrifice is praising God before and even if the miracle never comes.

Sometimes when we give a good report, our good report is a choice to sacrifice the reality of what you see, what you hear, and what you feel for the reality of the truth of what God's Word says. You replace the words that would naturally become the fruit of your lips with God's Word. God's Word is more powerful and more moving to you than what you see and sense with your own feelings. Begin to give God a sacrifice of praise, even now.

If the doctor says, "You're sick," choose to say aloud, "God, I thank you that you are my healer." If the bank manager says, "You're broke," choose to say aloud, "Lord, I thank you that you are Jehovah-Jireh. You are my provider." (And work your tail off to do your part in fixing the financial deficit.) If your marriage counselor gives no hope for your marriage, or your children are away from God, you give a good report. In faith, you declare, "God is in control. God will see us through. God is a Father to the generations of those who love Him."

These are just a few examples of real problems and the power of a good report response. Unfortunately, Some people are more rehearsed in the specifics of their illnesses than they are the Word of God. Some people know the names and even the proper Latin spelling of their affliction and can tell you who the top medical specialists are all over the country, but they can't recite a single scripture for healing. This behavior limits God. We are called to be overcomers, and we are directed to give a good report. When we give a good report in spite of negative circumstances, other people become inspired. They hear our positive words, and they are drawn to us. They wonder how we can keep speaking a good report. When we explain that it's God in us, we honor him, and we wear him well. We have accomplished the Lord's will when others are drawn to Him by our declarations of His goodness and mercy.

When we choose to give the good report during tough times, it honors God, and it blesses others. When we choose to give a good report, we are echoing the words of God. He has declared many powerful, victorious statements in His Word. Choose to repeat them, and you will come into greater alignment with His plan for your life. In so doing, your good report will honor Him, and you will be a great witness as a man or woman of God who wears Him well.

THE POWER OF A GOOD REPORT IN CHURCH LIFE

The Bible is full of examples of people whose lives teach us the power of a good report. The Word of God instructs us to use our words to stay "up" in an upside-down world.

A great example is the story of the Shunamite woman. As the story goes, this woman from Shunam served Elisha, the prophet of God. She was married and built a guestroom in her home for Elisha to rest as he traveled. She and her husband had no son. God blessed her faithfulness, and she had a son, as Elisha prophesied.

Tragically, the son died while still a boy. Now, this woman was older, and this was likely going to be her only child. It's hard to overstate the heartbreak she must have felt. Yet she knew the power of a good report. She went to tell Elisha, and the first words out of her mouth when he inquired of her state of mind was "All is well."[97] When he pressed her further and specifically asked, "How is your son?" she replied, "All is well."[98]

Her courage and resolve to trust in the Lord was extraordinary. She continued to profess that all was well, even as her son lay dead! In the end, Elisha came to her son, and God used Elisha to raise her son from the dead! I believe that her good report sustained her faith and allowed this miracle to occur. Miracles take place in an environment of faith. Jesus demonstrated this in the New Testament when he came to see Jairus's daughter, another young person who lay dead. Even Jesus, the Son of God, knew that a miracle couldn't happen in an atmosphere of doubt.

He entered Jairus's house, and the people in the room were crying and weeping. Jesus said, "Why all this commotion and wailing? The child is not dead but asleep."[99] The Bible says that the people laughed at Jesus. Jesus commanded all the people to leave the room. He couldn't tolerate the lack of faith and the absence of a good report. He went to the girl and commanded her to get up—and she was raised from the dead!

These lessons are powerful and instructive for how to live today. One of my life's messages is the power of a good report. I believe how we speak determines the outcome of our life. I believe it's truly a matter of life and death. The words that we use—whether a good report or a bad report—will shape our future.

During the financial crisis and economic meltdown of 2008-2009, I believe this message proved itself. I told our church, "I've made a decision about the recession. I'm not joining it!" You see, a real leader is someone who stays positive in tough circumstances. Real leadership is knowing the power of a good report and refusing to allow the negative reports of the world to bring us down. We must lift our faith through our words.

As a result of my encouragement and the faith that comes through a good report, several business leaders in our church chose to fight through the tough times, and they have reaped a tremendous growth in their businesses as a result.

One man in particular, with his partner, started a private mortgage company in this period. During the mortgage meltdown, they went into the mortgage business! That's gutsy, but that's faith. They knew the industry, they worked hard, and they always kept speaking a good report.

Recently, he presented a plaque to me, thanking me for the teaching of our church. Through trusting God and following the vision of a good report, that company has been profiled in national magazines and is now a billion-dollar business. The power of a good report overcomes the negative voices, but it also provides God's perspective in tough situations.

DEVELOP THE POWER OF A GOOD REPORT

PHASE 1: BEGIN SPEAKING AND THINKING ABOUT
THE GOOD THINGS IN LIFE.

PHASE 2: LEARN TO BE GOOD WITH GOOD.

PHASE 3: SEEK TO BUILD RELATIONSHIPS
WITH PEOPLE WHO GIVE A GOOD REPORT.

1. Do you think on good things? Do you actively seek opportunities to reflect on God's goodness in your life?
2. What is the typical response of people to your presence? What is the mirror of society telling you about your own self-perceptions?
3. How good is your fruit? Are you giving a good report so that the fruit of your lips honors God?
4. Do you have friends that are withered branches, or are they fruitful and alive? Do you need to change your environment as you seek to build the habit of giving a good report?

THE WILL OF GOD

Do not be conformed to this world, but be transformed by the renewing of your mind, that you may prove what is that good and acceptable and perfect will of God.

Romans 12:2

Everyone wants to know God's will. It is just as important to know what God's will isn't. I believe it is God's will for us to bear fruit, to be healed, and to be whole. While God's will is ever unfolding and even unpredictable, I believe it is difficult to be outside of God's will. When you are in God's will, you receive unexplainable strength to do His work.

True holiness consists of doing God's Will with a smile.

—Mother Teresa

IT'S JUST AS IMPORTANT TO KNOW
WHAT GOD'S WILL ISN'T

The desire of man to precisely know God's will has existed throughout human history. King Solomon expressed his frustration with being able to understand God and His will by writing the book of Ecclesiastes. After struggling to figure out why things happen, he begins by proclaiming in exasperation, "Everything is meaningless!"[100] Of course we know life is not meaningless, but the search to fully understand God's will can create such frustration that even the wisest man who ever lived essentially said, "I quit!"

Though even Solomon felt disturbed with the search to know God's will, we can at least take comfort in understanding the value of following His plan. We do this by perseverance. St. Frances De Sales, who lived from 1567-1622, wrote:

> And although the difficulties, temptations and the variety of circumstances which occur in the course of executing our [plan] might cause us some doubt as to whether we had made a good choice, yet we must remain settled, and not regard all this, but consider that if we had made another choice we had perhaps been a hundred times worse. Indeed, to say nothing of our not knowing whether it be God's will that we should be exercised in consolation or desolation, in peace or war.

As the previous quote highlights, we may not always feel complete confidence in a decision we've made, but we can always identify alternatives that would have been much worse, even wrong. I believe we can understand God's will in part by knowing what the will of God is not. There are many times when a "no" is as good as a "yes." In our church, we have an expression: "A good idea is not necessarily a God idea." A good idea could be a distraction from the God idea. You can spend your time doing things that are good, but those things can dilute your strength from doing the things that are from God.

There was a young man in our church who approached me about understanding God's will. He had gotten saved in jail and had just been released from prison. He was passionate about the future and wanted to go off to Bible college. I encouraged him to wait a bit. I said, "Look, mate, I love you, but you're not ready for that right now. Why don't you just get into church, pay off some of your debts, get yourself a job, and get some stability in your life? Spend some time serving in the church here." I believed that God had called him and given him a vision to reach the lost, but he needed to establish some credibility and gain some wisdom before he ran out to start a church!

Of course he resented my advice. He felt like I was holding him back from the call of God in his life, and he went off to Bible college in spite of my comments. Unfortunately, after he had been there just a short while, he floundered and struggled with managing all the responsibilities of the program. There was nothing wrong with him, and nothing wrong with eventually attending Bible college. He just wasn't ready. When we spoke, I had no agenda for him other than his best. And he came back several years later, with no real fruit of ministry in his life. He actually came to me and apologized and said, "You were right. I should have listened to you. I should have waited until I was mature enough to enter the program at Bible college."

I don't share that story to prove that I am good at giving advice. I share it because an important aspect of understanding what God's will is not, is realizing the importance of timing. As leaders, I believe we can save people from heartache and even lost years by helping them understand the importance of timing. We must always include in our counsel about God's will a clear explanation of what *God's will is not*.

GOD'S WILL IS UNFOLDING

It's great to know what God's will isn't. It's just as great to know God's will. In Colossians 1:9, the apostle Paul shares, "Since the day we heard it, we do not cease to pray for you and to ask that you may be filled with the knowledge of His will in all wisdom and spiritual understanding." Paul would not pray for something that could not be known. We can be filled with the knowledge of God's will. I believe it is an ongoing filling, which is why Paul did not cease to pray for it. His will is an unfolding development in our daily lives.

In my own life, I have seen the unfolding will of God continually amaze me. I never dreamed when I first gave my life to Jesus that I would be the pastor of a church in Virginia Beach, traveling the globe as God has allowed me to do and having an influence on people's lives through television and media. While I didn't know the specific details, I always had a sense that God wanted to use me to preach the gospel. It's a lot like the experiences of the children of Israel. God told them that He would give them the Promised Land, but He would give it to them little by little, because it would be too much for them to receive it all at once. It would have overwhelmed them. Likewise, I think if any of us understood from the beginning to the end of our lives what the will of God is for our lives, we would be quite overwhelmed, and we would likely become afraid to attempt what He had for us to do.

THE WILL OF GOD IS TO BEAR FRUIT

I can help anybody know what the will of God is for their life, the individual, specific will of God for their life in light of this Scripture. I begin with the premise that it is God's will that we bear fruit in every good work.[101] We all have good works in common that we are all called to do. We all are called to bear fruit in our marriage. We're all called to bear fruit in our finances. We're all called to bear fruit in our social life. We're all called to bear fruit in our church life. We're all called to bear fruit in our vocational life—in other words, our job. These are areas that every person has as a part of his life.

Within these common areas, we all have an area or two that is a great strength. Typically, we are strong and bearing fruit in the area we enjoy most, or in the area for which we have passion. Unfortunately, we also have areas that are more difficult for us to bear fruit. I've seen people that are bearing fruit in church life, but their marriage and family is suffering. After a while, in order to rescue their family, they'll pull out of church life to get their marriage and family right. I can understand why people have done that. Some of us have seen terrible leadership examples in church. Early on, I was taught that I needed to put my family on the altar and just serve God and just trust that God will take care of your family. I bitterly disagree with that teaching. I do not believe that is the will of God at all. I do not believe in a descending order of life priorities. The expression that we've all heard—God first, family second, job third, etc., is just wrong.

The problem then becomes a perpetual chasing to improve the area that was most recently neglected. People bounce back and forth, trying to strengthen their family (which is right), then trying to strengthen their job (which is right), then trying to bear fruit in church (which is also right). There is a balance in the will of God. He designed us to bear fruit in every good work. I believe it's the will of God to bear fruit in every area of our life all at the same time. If your marriage needs strengthening, take the time to strengthen your marriage along the way so that you don't abandon the area(s) that is bearing fruit and thereby never progress to any higher levels of fruitfulness.

We've got to bear fruit in every good work. I use a simple scoring table, which is located at the end of this chapter. After you've finished reading, please score yourself. It's easy—the scale is from one to five, with five being excellent and one being poor. So if your family life is a five and your church life is a two, you might want to get the fruit in your church life up to a three or four without sacrificing the area, the five, that is your family. It's not the will of God that we have one area prospering and doing well while other areas are suffering. It is the will of God for us to bear fruit in every area of life.

IT'S GOD'S WILL FOR US TO BE HEALED

"Now this is the confidence that we have in Him, that if we ask anything according to His will, He hears us. And if we know that He hears us, whatever we ask, we know that we have the petitions that we have asked of Him."[102]

John writes these words as a reminder to us. We are to be confident that God hears and He answers, when we ask according to His will. The obvious question then is, "Is it God's will for us to be healed?"

My answer to that question is an emphatic, "Yes!" Of course it's God's will for us to be healed. If it wasn't, then why did Jesus die on the cross? Only for our salvation? No. He bore our infirmities. By his stripes we were healed.[103] I have heard people pray, "God, if it's Your will, please heal this person." There's no reason to add the clause, "If it's Your will." It is His Will for everyone to be healthy and whole. John encourages us to be confident that He hears us and He answers. When you pray for healing, ask boldly, because we have confidence that He hears.

The timing of His healing is another matter altogether. We fully trust God and believe it is His will for healing, but what happens when a person doesn't get healed? What happens when they die without healing? I'm reminded of the trials of Shadrach, Meshach, and Abednego in the book of Daniel. They were found guilty of not bowing to the giant golden idol that King Nebuchadnezzar built. Everyone in Babylon was supposed to worship it or they would be thrown into a fiery furnace. As the three young men stood before the king just before being tossed into the fire, they said, "Our God is able to deliver us from the burning fiery furnace, and He will deliver us from your hand, O king. But if not, let it be known that we will not serve your gods or worship the golden image that you have set up!"[104]

Just as Daniel's friends knew it was possible and believed that God would deliver them, we must know it is possible and believe that God will heal. And, just as they professed to King Nebuchadnezzar, even if God didn't rescue them, He is still God. He is still worthy of worship and honor. Even if He doesn't heal in the way we expect, He's still God.

It is the will of God for you to walk through challenges and trials and persecutions, but you will come out the other side better and stronger than you went in. Shadrach, Meshach, and Abednego said our God is able to deliver us, but even if He doesn't, He is still God. They went through the fiery furnace, but God brought them out the other side, and the only thing that burnt in the furnace were their robes, the things that had them in bondage.

It is not the will of God for you to be sick. It is not the will of God for you to be poor. It takes no faith to be poor. I've heard Casey Treat, a great pastor from Seattle, say, "One of the best ways we can help the poor is not to be one of them." The Bible says that He takes pleasure in the prosperity of His people. The Bible says, "by His stripes we are healed." We can have confidence in Him to be healed, to be prosperous, because it is His will.

IT'S HARD TO LIVE OUTSIDE GOD'S WILL

I live my life as if I'm in the will of God. I think a person has to be stubborn and rebellious to live outside of God's will. I think it's harder to live outside the will of God than it is to live inside the will of God. The analogy that works best for me is comparing life to a sport. I'm a big fan of sports, and I enjoy cheering on great athletes in competition. In every sport—whether it is soccer, rugby, football, baseball, cricket, etc.—there is an umpire. The umpire stands on the field, but he isn't playing the game. He is there to enforce the rules. If you play within the rules, theoretically, you could play an entire game without the umpire's intervention. In life, once we know the rules, we can play or make decisions without having to ask the umpire's permission. We can't see this umpire, however, so how do we know if we've broken a rule or if he's blown his whistle? We know by His peace.

In Colossians 3:15 we read, "Let the peace of God *rule* in your hearts" (emphasis added). And that word *rule* comes from a Greek word βραβευω (pronounced "bra-byu-o") that means *umpire*. The peace of God is the umpire of your life. When you're in the middle of the game, so long as you don't hear a whistle, so long as you are at peace, you can keep playing. One thing is certain, you'll never hear from the umpire if you aren't playing. An umpire doesn't really care or is not concerned about spectators that are sitting up in the grandstands watching a game. He's only interested in the participants. When I ask people, "What do you want to do, what's the will of God for your life?" they'll say, "I just want to do God's will." I say, "Get involved." If we aren't playing the game, we'll never know God's will.

Twothirds of God's name is "Go." You'll never know what the will of God is until you get involved in something. If you've got a heart for children's ministry, start volunteering. If you have a passion for the arts, start participating in drama. Whatever you feel compelled to do in life, go after it. If the umpire blows his whistle, and you lose your peace, you'll know that's not the place for you. But you will never know the will of God until you get involved. Let the peace of God rule your heart.

If you follow this simple principle, you will find it very difficult to be outside of God's will.

Years ago, Sharon had a job that required her to travel forty-five minutes by train every day, one way! By the time she walked to the train station, her total travel time for a round trip was close to two-and-a-half hours. We were a busy couple: we were youth pastoring, and we began asking God for her to actually have a job that was local. We prayed that God would give her a short commute. We prayed for her to not only get a job that was close but also with better money, and better working conditions.

After applying, praying, and pleading, we believed God answered our prayers! She found a job as a legal secretary in the attorney general's office in Penrith, Australia. It was only ten minutes from our home. She supervised a group of court clerks and the court monitors. It paid better money. It had nicer working conditions. In every way, it appeared to be a much better job than her last one. But the moment she started working, she lost all peace. Now, it wasn't the fear of the unknown, or apprehension about a new environment. It was more than that. It was the peace of God, serving as the umpire, ruling her heart. It was like the Holy Spirit blew His whistle and said, "Stop playing—you're out of bounds." It was a flag being thrown on the field. She lost her peace, and she soon realized she was not supposed to take the job, even though it seemed to be everything we were praying for.

Sharon, to her credit, was obedient. She listened to the umpire. After only a week, she went back to her old boss and said, "Look, I've made a mistake. I'm sorry, but I just have no peace about this." And the boss actually said, "I was hoping you would change your mind." And she was able to keep her old job, with the agonizingly long commute and the lowered pay. But as soon as she returned, all her peace returned. The umpire said, "Play ball, you're back in the field!"

WORKING IN THE WILL OF GOD GIVES YOU STRENGTH

The following adaptation of the story of Jesus and the Samaritan woman shows how doing the will of God strengthens and refreshes you—even more than earthly food. In John 4, we read about Jesus, tired from his journey. He is alone, having sent the disciples into the city to find food. Along comes a social outcast, an adulterous Samaritan woman. Little did she know that day she would meet Jesus, who was doing God's will. And her world would be forever changed.

Jesus: I am very tired. Can you please get me a drink?

Woman: Are you asking me? I'm a Samaritan. Your people don't talk to mine.

Jesus: Your people? My people? Trust me, if you knew who I was, you would ask me for a drink, and I would give you water you never drank before, the water of life.

Woman: What? This is a really deep well, and you don't even have a bucket, much less a rope! Where is this water of life? This is Jacob's Well, the greatest well known to man! Are you greater than our father, Jacob, that you have some better source of water?

Jesus: No disrespect to Jacob, but whoever drinks from his well will eventually get thirsty again. But, get this—the water that I can give you? If you drink from that water, it will become like springs of eternal life within you!

Woman: Oh my god! Then please, give me this water! Then I won't have to draw from this well, and I won't have to come back here in shame and try to avoid all the people who think they are better than me!

Jesus: Okay. But first why don't you go get your husband?

Woman: I'm not married.

Jesus: I know. But you've been married before—five times. And now you're just living with a guy instead of being married.

Woman: How did you know that? You must be a prophet! I have worshiped sometimes, and our fathers worship on this mountain, but you Jews say that we are supposed to worship in Jerusalem. I'm not allowed there.

Jesus: Before you know it, even now, the time is coming when you won't have to worship God on this mountain, or even in Jerusalem. You will worship Him anywhere, because true worship happens in the spirit, and in truth. In fact, God is spirit, and He is looking for such to worship Him. And the time to worship Him is now.

Woman: Well, I do believe the Messiah will come. The Christ. When He comes, He will explain all of this to us.

Jesus: Daughter. I am He.

The Disciples return at this point. They are puzzled that Jesus is talking to this Samaritan woman, but none of them says anything.

Woman: I have to go!

The Samaritan woman runs off, leaving her water pot, because she is in such a hurry to tell the people in her city that she met the Messiah.

Disciple: Jesus, our teacher, you should eat. We brought you this food.

Jesus: I have eaten food that you don't know about.

Disciples (to each other): Did someone already bring Him food?

Jesus: My food is to do My Father's will, to finish His work. I have heard you comment that there are still four months before the harvest. Listen, I am now saying, look around. Look at the fields. They are ripe and ready to harvest! And everyone plays a part in the harvest—one reaps the harvest and gets paid, but the one who sows the seeds owns it and gains fruit for eternity! But both of them rejoice together, because the harvest meets their needs! Now do you understand the expression, "One sows and another reaps"? I sent you to reap for that which you have not labored. Others have worked hard, and now you get to enter into their nearly completed labor and get the benefits!

By now, the Samaritans have started to arrive, spurred on by the irresistible passionate testimony of a low-class, desperate, adulterous woman. So the Samaritans compelled Jesus to stay, and he remained for two days. And hundreds, perhaps thousands believed because they heard Him speak the words of life.

Samaritan citizens (to the woman): Now we believe, not because of what you said, for we ourselves have heard Him, and we know that this is indeed the Christ, the Savior of the world.⊠

The exchange between Jesus and the woman at the well is beautiful in many ways. The power of Jesus' words, the conversion of the Samaritan woman, the revival in the community—all are points about which sermons have been preached and books have been written. But the point I want to emphasize from this passage is that Jesus was satisfied by working in God's will even when his physical body was weak, tired, hungry, and thirsty.

Jesus was exhausted. There's a good chance that his natural body didn't have any desire to talk to anyone. He just wanted to get refreshed. And yet, He engaged in conversation with the woman, even though His natural body wanted to retreat and relax, because that was God's will. As a result of that conversation, that woman's life was transformed. The community experienced a great revival.

During this exchange, the disciples were gone. They had entered the city to get food. When the disciples finally returned, they urged Him to eat. They were concerned for Him. They had seen His humanity; they had witnessed His need for physical sustenance. Yet Jesus said, "I have meat to eat that you know not of…my food is to do the will of God and to finish His work."[106] He showed them that when you operate in the will of God, when you function in your calling, you are given spiritual sustenance that surpasses your immediate physical needs. In other words, if we're doing the will of God, we get energized. The will of God gives us strength. We have food to eat that people know not of.

I believe there are many pastors serving as the senior pastor when they are really gifted to be a staff pastor. They are called to be on a great team, but they are not designed to be the head pastor. I believe this is one of the reasons why some people experience burnout.

They are trying to do the will of God, and yet they're not gifted for the position they are trying to fill. It's draining and frustrating to try to be someone you're not. On the other hand, it's amazing how when you operate in the will of God, using your gifts, you receive strength. You receive "food" that people do not know about. Just as Jesus received power, energy, and vitality from operating in the will of God with His ministry to the woman at the well, when we operate in God's will, we gain strength.

THE WILL OF GOD IN CHURCH LIFE

As a young pastor, I recall having various people prophesy over my life. Many of us think that God is going to declare His will through an oracle. This can be dangerous. Within a span of a year, I had a prophet proclaim that I would go to cities in Australia. Then another one declared I was destined for New Zealand. Another prophet said the call of God for me was to go to Canada. I remember thinking God must be a schizophrenic if God was saying all these things. Of course God wasn't saying all those things. Those were men and women with sincere hearts trying to encourage me. Which is why we must judge prophets. If someone prophesies over you and it doesn't resonate, sit right in your spirit; the best thing to do is to put it in a place of abeyance, to put it on the shelf. If it's God, he'll bring it to pass, and if it's not, then you don't want to try and make that happen.

A young lady in our church once had someone prophesy over her that God had called her to Japan. She was fairly new to our church and fairly new to the Lord, and she just took off and moved to Japan. We tried to encourage her to be patient. We encouraged her to remain planted and grow—*burden doesn't necessitate timing*. Just because someone prophesied doesn't mean we should act. A person must take the time to seek counsel and wisdom. So that young girl went prematurely without the blessing of the house, without the prayers and covering of the church. She launched out to Japan without any training or structure. After awhile she came back and had nothing great to report of anything God did. If we aren't careful, we can fall prey to the same temptation. We receive encouragement or get a vision for something, and we take off without any development or strategy.

In the Old Testament, there is a story of a messenger who committed the same foolish behavior. The Bible says when the messenger arrived, the Cushite, he was told by David to step aside until the person who had the whole message could deliver the whole message. In 2 Samuel 18, the story is told of the death of Absalom, King David's son. Joab, the captain of David's army, selects Cushi, a messenger, to go with the letter to David, notifying the king of the tragedy of his son's death. Cushi takes off, running to the king, who is several miles away. Shortly thereafter, Ahimaaz, another messenger, approaches Joab and asks if he can run to King David.

The message was secret, because the king was at war. Ahimaaz didn't have any message to take to David. Joab explained to him that there was no message to take, that Cushi had left with the message. Ahimaaz insisted on running to King David.

It sounds foolish, but how often do we take off running without having the full message to give to people? How often do people sprint out to the mission field without fully having the power of God operating in their life? Many times, I've unfortunately seen people invest without a clear strategy. I've seen people start businesses without a business plan. They run without a course or a message!

Now, Ahimaaz was fast. And he caught and passed Cushi. He arrived at the palace first, and the guards were happy to receive him. King David remarked, "He is a good man, and comes with good tidings"[107] Little did David know, but Ahimaaz had *no tidings*.

Ahimaaz entered the palace and was received by King David. He stands there alone, with the entire royal court waiting to hear about the news from the battle—about Absalom, his dear son.

King David asks him what happened at the battle, and Ahimaaz just stands there. He mutters something about how the battle was ferocious, but that he didn't know what happened. Can you imagine David's frustration? Even his anger? He was expecting great news from this messenger—instead he got an "I don't know."

Too often I see people in the church, desperate to know God's will, race out to some mission or charitable effort without any preparation. It is God's will for you to be playing in the game, but you can't play the game without knowing any of the rules or even being able to identify the ball.

Don't run without a message. Trust God to work in your life in the church where you're planted. When it's time to run, He'll be sure you have the right message for His people. Don't chase the "will of God." Chase God and live as though you are in His will—because it's very likely that you are.

DETERMINE HOW YOU ADD UP IN GOD'S WILL

I want to encourage you to take the time right now to do an assessment on yourself. Using the table below, rate yourself from one to five, and use the full gambit of numbers. Don't just use twos and threes and fours. If you're really prospering in your finances and you've got that under control, if you're tithing and you're living within your means, give yourself a five. But if you've got more debt and credit cards and you're upsidedown and you don't have a dollar to give if God told you to give it, give yourself a one. List those things from one to five, and look at all the ones and twos, and see there the will of God for you. That is the revealed will of God—that you need to get those areas strengthened now in your life without sacrificing the areas where you are bearing fruit.

Score	Family	Finances	Social	Church	Job	Health
5 – Excellent						
4 – Very Good						
3 – Average						
2 – Fair						
1 – Poor						

NOTES

THE ACCENT OF LEADERSHIP

1. Gupta, Anthea Fraser. "Ask a linguist FAQ." http://linguistlist.org/ask-ling/accent.cfm

2. John 11:43

3. Proverbs 18:21

4. Matthew 6:9-10

5. John 17

6. 1 Peter 2:11

7. Polybius; McGing, Brian. *The Histories.* Oxford: Oxford University Press, 2010.

8. Suetonius. (Translated by J.C. Rolfe) *The Lives of the Caesars – Julius. Augustus. Tiberius. Gaius. Caligula.* Cambridge, MA: Harvard University Press, 1914.

9. 1 Peter 4:11

HONOR

10. Psalm 75:5-7, Daniel 2:20-21, Proverbs 21:1

11. Numbers 12:4-10

12. Luke 2:41-50

13. Proverbs 10:12: "love covers all sins."

14. Hebrews 13:17

15. 1 Timothy 5:17

16. Proverbs 3:9

THE RESTRAINTS OF VISION

17. Mallet, Clifford John and Hanrahan, Stephanie. "Elite Athletes: What makes the fire burn so brightly?" *Psychology of Sport and Exercise* Volume 5, Issue 2(April 2004): 183-200.

18. 1 Corinthians 12:12-31

19. John 12:32

20. The incentive to undertake an activity based on the expected enjoyment of the activity itself; personal satisfaction derived through self-initiated achievement.

21. Proszenko, Adrian. "Golden Boy Phelps guns for Thorpe." Sydney Morning Herald February 13, 2011.

22. Ibid.

23. Genesis 25:31-33

24. Judges 14:9

25. Judges 16:20

26. Matthew 28:16-20

27. Luke 2:41-51

28. Hebrews 10:25

29. Matthew 16:18-20

30. John 10:10

31. Joshua 24:15

FAVOR

32. Revelation 20:11-15

33. 1 Peter 4:17

34. Psalm 107

35. Matthew 16:25

36. Genesis 30:27

37. Luke 15:1-7

38. 2 Thessalonians 1:8-9

39. John 6:64

THE HOLY SPIRIT

40. Luke 3:22

41. Exodus 16, Numbers 11:4-10

42. Matthew 16:4

43. Hebrews 11:6

44. John 21:25

45. Mark 16:17-20

46. Revelation 22

47. Luke 9:35

48. Acts 2:3

49. John 14:26

50. 1 Corinthians 14:40

51. 1 Kings 19:11-13

52. 1 Corinthians 14:33

53. Acts 2:9-11

54. Romans 8:28

YOUR DESTINY IS CONNECTED TO YOUR LEADER

55. Luke 7:28

56. Matthew 11:1-6

57. Matthew 3:13-17

58. John 1:29

59. Matthew 3:3

60. John 1:19-27

61. Luke 1:36

62. Matthew 11:4-6

63. Psalm 84:10

64. Exodus 2:1-8

65. Exodus 2:11-12

66. Exodus 2:13-14

67. Exodus 3

68. Numbers 12:11-12

69. Numbers 12:13-14

70. Acts 9:26-29

71. Acts 15:36-41

HAVE YOU COME TO HELP?

72. Matthew 16:18

73. 1 Chronicles 12:8

74. 1 Chronicles 12:17

75. 1 Chronicles 12:19

A SPIRIT OF EXCELLENCE

76. Genesis 6-8

77. Genesis 2:9

78. Proverbs 19:15

79. Luke 16:10

80. Proverbs 26:16

81. Exodus 32

82. Exodus 32:7-14

83. Exodus 32:25

THE POWER OF A GOOD REPORT

84. Philippians 4:8

85. Ibid.

86. Proverbs 3:27

87. Matthew 12:34

88. Exodus 13:1

89. Exodus 13:17

90. Exodus 13:23

91. Exodus 13:33

92. Exodus 14:9

93. Maxwell, John C. *Winning with People*, Nashville, TN: Thomas Nelson Publishers, 2004.

94. Proverbs 12:14

95. Proverbs 18:20

96. Matthew 4:4

THE WILL OF GOD

97. 2 Kings 4:23

98. 2 Kings 4:26

99. Mark 5:39

100.   Ecclesiastes 1:1

101.   Colossians 1:10

102.   1 John 5:14-15

103.   Isaiah 53:5

104.   Daniel 3:17-18

105.   John 4:1-42

106.   John 4:32, 34

107.   2 Samuel 18:27